TOM BRADY

LADAINIAN TOMLINSON

RICHARD J. BRENNER

EAST END PUBLISHING, LTD.
Huntington, New York

AUTHOR'S NOTE: Tom Brady and LaDainian Tomlinson are gifted athletes, but they both had to work hard and overcome many obstacles before they were able to achieve their dreams. And, even now, they keep working on their games, trying to become the best players that they can be.

"It's never come easy for me," said Tom Brady. "I was always the one that no one ever picked. The only way I ever got to where I wanted to go was to work as hard as I could."

You can achieve your dreams, too, if you believe in yourself and work as hard to achieve your goals as Brady and Tomlinson work to achieve theirs. And there are lots of areas for you to consider besides athletics. You might want to become an artist or a musician or a writer; or you might decide to work for world peace or to help clean the environment. The real lesson to be learned is that you can accomplish whatever you put your mind to, as long as you're willing to work hard to achieve it.

This book is dedicated, as all my books are, to the children of the world. I wish that all of you could live in peaceful, loving surroundings, free from fear and bigotry of every type.

savedarfur.org

I also want to express great appreciation to everybody whose time and talents have contributed to this book, including Mark Cohen, Janie DeVos, John Douglas, Jon Backus, Bob Christoper, Walter Satterthwait, Jim Wasserman, Jamie Calsyn, Ellen Raimondo Shupp and Rob Tringali. I also want to express sincere thanks to Ed Masessa and Janet Speakman.

Copy Editor: John Douglas   **Assistant Copy Editor: Walter Satterthwait**
Research Editor: Janie DeVos   **Book Design: Studio 31, Inc.**

Photo Credits: **SportsChrome** supplied the following images, with photographers' names in parenthesis: P.66 and 68 (**Rob Tringali**); P.73 (**Bryan Yablonsky**); P.75 (**Michael Zito**). The TCU Athletic Department supplied the photograph on P 74. Icon SMI supplied all of the remaining photographs, as per the following: P.65 (**Rick Kane**); P.67 (**Jerome Davis**); P.69 (**Albert Dickson/TSN/ZUMA Press**); P.70 and P.77 (**Ed Wolfstein**) P.72 and the cover image of Tom Brady (**Douglas Jones**); P.76 (**Stan Lui**); P.78 (**Kevin Reece**); P.79 (**Matt A. Brown**); P.80 and LaDainian Tomlinson cover photograph (**Scott Sewell**).

ISBN: 0-943403-72-3

Published by EAST END PUBLISHING, LTD.
112 Abbott Dr.
Huntington, NY 11743
Printed in the United States of America by R.R. Donnelley

Richard J. Brenner, America's best-selling sportswriter, has written more than 80 exciting sports titles. For details on how to order some of them, see the back page of this book.
***
Mr. Brenner is also available to speak at schools and other venues. For details, including fees, you may e-mail him directly at: rjbrenner1@gmail.com, or write to him c/o EEP, 112 Abbott Dr. Huntington, NY 11743.

AUTHOR'S MESSAGE: For many years, Native American groups have been appealing to sports teams not to use names and logos that many Native American people find offensive, such as "Redskins." Out of respect for, and in support of those appeals, I have chosen not to use such names in this book, except for those names of tribes, such as Seminoles, which relevant Indian groups have authorized. I urge all readers who agree with this position to write to the owner of the Washington team, Dan Snyder, and to Roger Godell, the commissioner of the National Football League, and add your voice to those who are protesting the use of those names and logos.

TABLE OF CONTENTS

TOM BRADY

LADAINIAN TOMLINSON

1   NEVER PICKED

Tom Brady came into the world on August 3, 1977, the youngest of Galynn and Tom Sr.'s four children, and their only son. He was raised in San Mateo, California, a comfortable and affluent suburb located about 30 miles south of San Francisco.

Brady grew up in a house with a close-knit, loving and supportive family that was athletically talented and enthusiastic about competition. His mother, Galynn, is an excellent tennis player and a fine golfer; while his father, Tom Sr., is also an avid golfer and an occasional basketball player. Each of Brady's three sisters played soccer and softball and Maureen, the eldest, was such a talented high school pitcher that she threw *14 perfect games,* which earned her a scholarship to Fresno State.

"I don't think we were typical girls," said Nancy, the youngest of the three sisters. "We liked to play everything the boys did, and there were about 80 or 90 kids in the neighborhood, so there was always something going on. And it was always the three Brady girls and Tommy."

Although Brady reveled in the neighborhood games, he was a slow runner and was never the best player, or even close.

"It's never come easy to me," said Brady. "I was always the one that no one ever picked. That's why I think I play with a chip on my shoulder. I have some scars that have never healed."

While Brady wasn't the fastest or most talented athlete, he was extremely competitive.

"When I was growing up, there was a kid in the neighborhood who was a lot faster than I was," recalled Brady. "I challenged him to a race. He killed me. I challenged him again. He killed me again. I just kept challenging him until I beat him. It's like the tortoise and the hare. I was the tortoise."

Although Brady's competitive nature is what pushed him to achieve success at every level that he has ever played at, it also, sometimes, sends him over the edge. When he was young, for example, whenever he lost a video game to the computer, he'd throw the remote against the television.

"I wound up breaking a TV and countless remotes," admits Brady, with a touch of embarrassment. "Finally, my mom just quit buying new ones for me."

When he was 8 years-old, Brady also lost it on the golf course after he hit a poor shot while playing his weekly round with his father. He slammed a club to the ground as hard as he could, which prompted his father to end the round on the spot.

"Get your butt in the cart, we're going home right now," said Brady's dad.

"I can lose it pretty good," said Brady. "But that's not something I'm proud of, and I'd like to change it."

In addition to being passionate participants in athletics, the Brady's were also fervent fans of the San Francisco 49ers football team. On autumn Sundays, when the Niners were playing at home, the family frequently spent the early part of the day tailgating at Candlestick Park, where the team played, before going in to watch the game.

One of Brady's earliest memories is of being in the stands when the 49ers rallied to beat the Dallas Cowboys in the 1981 NFC Championship game, 28-17. The star of the game was quarterback Joe Montana, who threw the game-winning touchdown pass to wide receiver Dwight Clark with less than a minute left to play. The win propelled the 49ers to the first of their five Super Bowl victories, while the pass was the launching pad for Montana's eventual entry into the Pro Football Hall of Fame. The only memory that Brady has of that game, however, is of his crying throughout the first half because his parents wouldn't buy him one of those oversized foam hands that proclaim the 49ers as being *No. 1*.

In the neighborhood football games that Brady played when he was older, he would always pretend to be Montana or Steve Young, the left-handed quarterback and future Hall of Famer who eventually replaced Montana and who led the 49ers to the last of their five Super Bowl titles.

"Every game we played, I was always Montana or Young, at least in my mind," said Brady, who also went to the 49ers Super Bowl victory parades in San Francisco. "The neighborhood driveways were my Candlestick Park."

Brady also had posters of a couple other Hall of Fame quarterbacks hanging on his bedroom wall, namely Denver Broncos' great John Elway, who won two Super Bowls, and the Miami Dolphins' Dan Marino, who set most of the NFL career passing records, but never won a

Super Bowl. Marino did get one chance at Super Sunday, but he ran into a red-hot Joe Montana, who had a record-setting MVP game while leading the 49ers past the Dolphins in Super Bowl XIX.

"Joe Montana was the one I really looked up to," said Brady. "If there was anybody I could be like, it would be Joe Montana. No question."

Although Brady's entire family enjoyed sports, and his parents had no objection to him playing neighborhood football games, they wouldn't allow him to play organized football until he entered high school, because they thought that the sport was too dangerous for younger children.

Interestingly, that was the same conclusion reached by the parents of a quarterback whose career would, in the future, frequently intersect with Brady's.

"I don't like the idea of organized tackle football for young kids," said former Pro Bowl quarterback Archie Manning, who didn't allow Peyton or either of his other two sons to play youth football. "It's too dangerous."

2 THE RIGHT VIBE

Brady attended Junipero Serra High School, an all-boys school that has sent a fair number of its graduates on to professional baseball, including shortstop Jim Fregosi, who went on to become a big league manager after his major league playing career was finished. Serra's most famous baseball-playing alumnus, however, is Barry Bonds, the San Francisco Giants' slugger, who has won seven National League MVP Awards. Bonds, who set the single-season record for home runs with 73 in 2001, will most likely surpass Hank Aaron's career home run record of 755 at some point during the 2007 season.

Although the school wasn't noted for turning out high-profile football players, there was one notable exception, Lynn Swann. Swann, an acrobatic wide receiver, won four Super Bowl rings with the Pittsburgh Steelers between the 1974 and 1979 seasons, and was inducted into the Pro Football Hall of Fame in 2001.

Brady joined the Serra freshman football squad as a ninth grader, and became the Padre's backup quarterback. His parents didn't have to worry about him being injured, though, since he didn't take a single snap, but just sat and watched as the Padres lost every game on their schedule. Brady took over as the starting quarterback for the junior varsity the following year, but only because the returning starter, his best friend, Kevin Krystofiak, decided to quit the team.

Although he got to play only because he was the default selection, Brady took advantage of the opportunity and started developing his quarterbacking skills. He passed accurately and effectively, connecting for 17 touchdown passes and only three interceptions, and was named to the first-team all-league junior varsity by the league's coaches.

Despite that level of success, Tom MacKenzie, Serra's varsity coach, told Brady that he would have to work harder and spend more time in the weight room if he had hopes of winning a college football scholarship.

"I don't think I ever had to tell him to work hard again," said MacKenzie. "Because he didn't start out as a superstar, he learned how important it was to keep learning and growing as an athlete. He also learned that he would have to struggle if he wanted to reach his goals."

Brady responded to the advice by working out with a personal trainer and attending summer football camps. When he went to the camp run by Tom Martinez, which he did for three years, he impressed the noted quarterback guru with his attentiveness, even more than with his talent.

"I've always said that people have two ears and one mouth, so they should listen twice as much as they talk," said Martinez. "But so many young kids don't want to listen. Tommy did. I'd talk, he would listen, and then he'd go and work at it. He worked his butt off and always believed in himself."

Working hard was almost second nature to Brady, who always believed that increased effort leads to faster improvement.

"I've always worked hard, and I've never minded

doing it," said Brady. "I was always working on trying to improve my speed. During the summers I would run just as hard as I could. I would always come in last, but I would keep trying and, eventually, I got a little bit faster and I also built up my stamina. I also lifted weights to increase the strength in my legs and my upper body. I did everything that I could to become the best quarterback that I could be."

When Brady returned to Serra for his junior year, MacKenzie selected him as the varsity's starting quarterback. The lanky junior had an effective, if not spectacular season, as he led the Padres to a 6-4 record and was named to the second-team all-county squad.

"I was still very far from being a great quarterback, but I had definitely improved," said Brady.

Back then, however, no one had a clue that Brady would win a football scholarship, let alone go on to the NFL. In fact, his best sport was baseball, and he was a well-regarded catching prospect. In the spring of his senior year at Serra, the Montreal Expos thought enough of his potential as a backstop to select Brady in the 18th round of the 1995 baseball draft.

"He hadn't shown any great promise as a football player at this point," recalled Rick Chandler, who had coached Brady's ninth grade basketball team. "But I just knew that, somehow, he would make it in whatever he chose to do. He was just too smart, too positive, and loved football too much to not be successful. He just had that vibe."

Although the Padres finished with a mediocre 5-5 mark in Brady's senior season, he was selected first-team All-Northern California and was rated one of the top 23 high school quarterbacks in the country by Super Prep magazine.

Thanks in part to his father, who had created a highlight tape of his best plays and sent copies to about 60 schools, Brady had a large list of scholarship offers, but eventually decided to accept one from the University of Michigan.

"I was lucky that I had choices coming out of high school, but I knew how hard I had worked to be in that position," said Brady. "I already had the size and arm strength, so I knew that if I worked hard enough and dedicated myself to playing, that I could make it."

Although Brady was about to leave his home and family, and swap California's pleasant climate for the often harsh winters of the Midwest, he still looks back with great fondness at the years he spent at Serra.

"I had a wonderful time in high school," said Brady. "I went to a great school, with tremendous academic support, a darned good baseball team and a pretty good football team. Going there helped me a lot when I started college."

3 PLAYING IN THE TALL GRASS

Under his picture in his high school yearbook, Brady had written what some people might consider to be a somewhat pompous phrase:

If you want to play with the big boys, you have to learn to play in the tall grass.

During his five-year stay at Michigan, the young quarterback would discover just how difficult and painful that process could be.

By the time he arrived at Ann Arbor to start his college career in the summer of 1995, the coach who had recruited him and the head coach who had approved the scholarship were no longer at Michigan.

"Nobody who I had established a relationship with was there, and I felt like a bit of an orphan," said Brady, who was 2,000 miles away from his family and living on his own for the first time in his life. "It was certainly a growing up experience, and I learned that I'd better grow up quick."

What Brady did find when he reported to his first football practice didn't make him feel any better, because he was at the bottom of the team's quarterback depth chart, behind six other talented signal-callers.

The Wolverines were so stocked at the position that Lloyd Carr, the new head coach, decided to red-shirt

Brady, which meant that he could practice with the team but he could not play at all in his freshman year at Michigan.

What made the situation seem even gloomier was that the players at the top of the chart were Scott Dreisbach, who was only one year ahead of Brady, and Brian Griese, who was two years ahead of him.

"I wasn't in a very good position," noted Brady, who began working as hard as he could to improve his game and his ranking. "It's not as though they were graduating seniors. I mean, I didn't have much of a chance unless one of those guys got hurt or I improved."

Brady moved up to third string the following year, but he felt as though he deserved to start, and expressed that thought to Lloyd Carr. When Carr told him that he had a long way to go before he'd be ready to start, Brady thought about transferring to a different school, one where he wouldn't be at the end of the line.

"I thought I had improved enough to play, but in looking back I realize that I wasn't ready at that point," said Brady, who decided to stick it out at Michigan. "There's so much more that goes into being a quarterback than throwing the football. You also need to have leadership skills, poise, and concentration. It's a learning process, or at least it was for me."

After a year spent working out, watching film, and practicing, Brady jumped ahead of Dreisbach and came within a hair's width of beating out Griese as the Wolverines' starter.

"When we broke camp, it was neck-and-neck between the two of them," said Stan Parrish, who was the team's quarterbacks coach. "You could have almost flipped a coin."

Given the chance, Griese went on to lead Michigan to an undefeated season, which he capped with an MVP performance in the Wolverines' 21-16 win over Washington in the 1998 Rose Bowl.

After Griese left for the NFL as the third round pick of the Denver Broncos in the 1998 draft, Brady won the battle with Dreisbach for the starting role the following fall. But he knew that his hold on the reins was tentative, because lurking in the wings was freshman phenom Drew Henson, who many people, including Lloyd Carr, thought was the next great quarterback.

"Obviously, Brady has an advantage because he's paid his dues," said Carr, in what was an underwhelming show of support. "But there's no question that Henson is the most talented quarterback ever to come to Michigan."

Although he knew that his hold on the job might be tenuous and that Carr could turn to Henson in a heartbeat, Brady had no intention of yielding what he had waited so long to achieve.

"To be the best, you have to beat out the best," said Brady. "I've fought long and hard to be in this position and I don't plan to give it up."

Brady got off to a shaky start, however, and the Wolverines, who had come into the season ranked No. 5 in the nation, dropped their first two games, 36-20 at Notre Dame, and then a 38-28 spanking by Syracuse before 110,000 disappointed fans in Ann Arbor.

"They were a big-time school and no one really gave

us a chance," said Donovan McNabb, who was the Syracuse quarterback. "But we got them down early and we kept them down."

In each of those two games, Henson had come in to mop-up, and he had wound up generating more offense than Brady had. In fact, it was the freshman who had come into the Syracuse game in the fourth quarter, and then proceeded to pilot the Wolverines to three of their four touchdowns.

"It was one of the low points for me," acknowledged Brady. "I have never been in a game where my team was so thoroughly dominated. Donovan was incredible. That was the worst defeat I've ever experienced.

"In regard to being pulled from the games, I can only control what I control, which is how I play," said Brady. "When Coach decides to put Drew in the game, I have to deal with that. When I do get called on to come in after Drew, I have to go out there and perform."

Which is exactly what Brady did, as he led the Wolverines to wins in 10 of their final 11 games, including a 45-31 come-from-behind win over Arkansas in the Citrus Bowl. It was a wonderful high note on which to end a season that had started off with two low ones.

"Of course, when you show what you can do out there, and you play well, it's a good feeling," acknowledged Brady, who had traveled a long and winding road to reach the success he finally achieved. "It's definitely more fun when things are going well."

Brady's play also seemed to impress his head coach, and made him look like a lock to return as the starter for his senior season.

"Tom's a bright guy, he has a good arm and his team-mates look up to him," said Carr. "I think he has the right stuff."

By the following autumn, however, Carr had decided that Brady, who had been elected one of the team's captains, would start the opening game and Henson would play the second quarter. Then, at halftime, Carr would decide whom to send in to start the second half.

It was a tough situation, especially for a senior who was down to his last season and his final attempt to progress as a player and attract the attention of NFL scouts. But Brady never pouted or grumbled about the decision.

"I'm not saying whether or not he liked it, but Tom never flinched, never complained," said Mike DeBord, who was the Wolverines' offensive coordinator. "He was handed a difficult situation and he handled it beautifully."

The Wolverines opened their 1999 schedule against Notre Dame for the second straight year, but this time Brady turned the tables on the Fighting Irish by rallying Michigan from a 14-point deficit to a 26-12 win. Although Carr continued to rotate his quarterbacks for the next six games, Brady went on to play at such a high level that the coach finally stopped the merry-go-round and put the team entirely in his senior's hands.

"Nothing was given to him," said quarterbacks' coach, Stan Parrish. "He earned everything he got."

With Brady at the wheel, the Wolverines rode to four straight wins to end the regular season with a 10-2 record.

"He never backed down from a challenge," said DeBord. "That's the thing that always impressed me about Tom."

Brady then finished his college career in a blaze of glory by completing 34 of 46 pass attempts for 369 yards and four touchdowns, as he led Michigan to a 35-34 overtime win against Alabama in the Orange Bowl.

As the Michigan players and coaching staff celebrated the exciting win, DeBord, who had decided to accept a coaching position at another school, sought out Brady amidst the pandemonium.

"I told him, 'Since I'm leaving Michigan, I was glad to be leaving with him,'" recalled DeBord. "That's not putting down any of the other Michigan quarterbacks that I'd coached, because there were some great ones; it was just my way of telling him that I put him on a higher pedestal."

In the end, even Lloyd Carr had come to appreciate the fact that Brady had not only achieved athletic success, but that he had done so with dedication and determination.

"He made believers out of everybody here," said Carr. "He represents everything that's positive about being an athlete."

Brady had come to Michigan as an untested seventh-stringer, but he left it as one of the top quarterbacks in the school's history. And through those five years of growth, as difficult as the process had often been, he learned that he could, indeed, play in the tall grass with the big boys.

4   FROM LAST TO FIRST

Although Brady had established himself as one of the top passers in Michigan history, and had also shown that he had the mental toughness to thrive in the midst of difficulty, NFL teams were less than overwhelmed with his potential to succeed in professional football.

"The big question that scouts had on him was why Michigan would try to play a freshman over him," said Tom Donahoe, who was the general manager of the Buffalo Bills. "That had everybody concerned."

The doubts went so deep that Brady wasn't selected until the sixth round of the 2000 draft, when he was finally picked by the New England Patriots after 198 other college players, including seven mostly forgotten quarterbacks, had already been chosen.

"When I went in the sixth round, it wasn't anything new for me," acknowledged Brady, who had almost grown used to being overlooked. "My whole college career had been about competition. I knew I just needed to slug it out."

When Brady arrived at his first training camp with the Pats, his position was similar to the one he had faced at Michigan. He was at the bottom rung of a ladder and he wasn't given any assurances about reaching the next rung, let alone moving all the way to the top one. What's more, this was the NFL, and Bill Belichick, New England's demanding head coach, hadn't given him a four-

year scholarship. If Brady hadn't shaped up quickly, Belichick wouldn't have had any reservations about releasing him and searching for another fourth-string quarterback.

Although he was playing behind three other signal-callers, and wasn't given all that much chance of rising higher, or getting any playing time, Brady focused his attention on every detail of his responsibilities and, even then, displayed a level of leadership that impressed his veteran teammates. When he thought he saw a better way for something to be done, he spoke up and offered his advice. But he also knew when to pick his spots and when to remain quiet.

"He's quick and observant," said center Ken Walter. "But he also knows when not to talk, and that's just as important."

He also devoted what seemed liked endless hours to memorizing the Pats' playbook and analyzing game film in order to familiarize himself with New England's offense and the tendencies of opposing defenses.

Once the season started, Brady spent almost every game day on the sidelines. In fact, he was inactive for all but two of the team's games, and wound up throwing only three passes in the one game in which he did receive a few minutes of playing time. It was a situation that Brady had no argument with.

"When I got here, I was so far from being an NFL quarterback," acknowledged Brady. "I wasn't strong enough or quick enough to play at that level."

Belichick had told Brady that the only way he would stick with the Pats past this first season would be for him to get quicker and stronger, and improve his passing mechanics. Brady heard the message loud and clear and was in the weight room every day during the season. In the following off-season, he participated in every one of the team's 60 workouts, even though most of them weren't mandatory.

By the time the team had reassembled in July to begin training for the 2001 season, Brady had added 15 pounds of muscle, which helped him to increase his arm strength, and he was also able to out-run teammates who he hadn't been able to keep up with a year earlier.

"At training camp you could see how much work he had put in during the off-season," said center Damien Woody. "His throwing mechanics were much smoother and, as practices went on, we started to get a good idea of what he might be capable of."

The coaching staff had also noted the big difference, and then they saw the results translated onto the field in Brady's performances during training camp and in the pre-season games. As a result, Brady was promoted to second-string over Damon Huard, whom the team had signed after he'd been released by the Miami Dolphins.

"We brought in Damon Huard to be our No.2 guy," said Charlie Weis, who was the Pats' offensive coordinator. "He had done a good job backing up Dan Marino down in Miami, and in training camp he was pretty good. But we saw things that made us decide to make Tom the No. 2. He showed us that he might turn out to be special."

Belichick, if anything was even more enthusiastic than Weis.

"I'm not sure I've ever seen any player improve as much as Tom has in such a short time," said Belichick.

"When he came to training camp, right away, everybody saw the dramatic improvement."

With his rapid development, Brady started the season on the bench, as the second banana behind Bledsoe, where he might have remained for the rest of the season. But, in the team's second game, Bledsoe suffered a serious injury when New York Jets' linebacker Mo Lewis decked him with a sickening hit.

"I still remember the way it sounded; it was like two cars crashing," said Brady. "It was two huge bodies running at full speed and Drew just got massacred."

The blow punctured an artery in Bledsoe's chest, and he was forced to leave the game and give way to Brady. But Brady wasn't able to jump-start the Pats' offense, and New England lost the game, 10-3, which dropped their record to 0-2.

The following week, New England won its first game of the season, a 44-13 wipeout of the Indianapolis Colts and Peyton Manning, their Pro Bowl quarterback. Although Brady didn't play a key role in the victory in terms of productivity, he didn't make any mistakes, either. Afterwards, Brady signed a game ball and sent it to Tom Martinez, which was his way of thanking his former tutor for helping him to get where he was.

The Pats reverted to their losing ways in Miami, however, as the Dolphins' defense stifled Brady and sent the New Englanders home with a 30-10 defeat. The season seemed to be slipping toward mediocrity, if not total disaster and, despite all the great press notices he'd received in training camp, Brady had looked ordinary in his first two starts. The New England fans who hadn't already given up on the 2001 season anxiously listened for news about Bledsoe's return, while those fans who had given the team up for dead, were left to count the days until the Boston Celtics tipped off the NBA season, and the Red Sox reported to spring training.

Their prospects seemed to dim still further the following week when the San Diego Chargers and their dynamic rookie running back, LaDainian Tomlinson, came to Foxboro and rocked the Pats back on their heels. With time getting tight in the fourth quarter, the visitors held a 26-16 lead and were already starting to think about an enjoyable return flight to the West Coast. But, Brady suddenly started to click and proceeded to connect on 13 of his final 19 passes, as he led the Pats on three consecutive scoring drives and to a 29-26 victory.

Brady, who had completed 33 of his 54 pass attempts and his first two NFL touchdown passes, was named the American Football Conference Player of the Week in only his third NFL start.

"His decision-making is a real strength," said Belichick. "He understands coverages and where the openings are going to be."

Brady sparkled again the following week in the Pats' second game of the season against the Colts, as he completed 80 percent of his attempts and threw a trio of TD passes in New England's 38-17 win in Indianapolis.

But he followed that dream game with a nightmarish one in Denver. The Pats not only lost the game, but Brady, who had thrown 162 passes without an interception, was picked off four times by the Broncos. His teammates and coaches knew that a performance like that had the potential to send a player, especially a young, untested quarterback, into mental paralysis.

But Brady erased those doubts by bouncing right back and throwing three touchdown passes with no interceptions in the team's next game, a 24-10 win over the Atlanta Falcons.

"I've had hard times before," said Brady, who refuses to allow a bad performance to knock him off his stride. "You learn how to deal with them and just move forward. You have to know how to put everything behind you, because you can't get last week back."

It was that mental toughness, as much as Brady's quarterbacking skills, which convinced Belichick to stick with him as the team's starter, even after Bledsoe had recovered from his injury.

Brady went on to reward his coach's decision by leading the team to six straight season-ending wins, which upped their record to 11-5 and earned them the AFC East title.

"I think at some point you have to sit back and evaluate and say, 'Wow, this has been a pretty good year,'" said Brady, in what qualifies as a pretty good understatement. "I don't think it's as much about how far I've come, but about how far we've come as an offense."

In his first season as a starter, Brady didn't merely stand in, he stood out, throwing for 2,843 yards and completing 63.9 percent of his passes, a franchise record. He had begun the season as an understudy, and finished it by being named to the Pro Bowl, only the fifth quarterback in NFL history to earn a trip to Hawaii in the season of his first start.

"If you look at everything he's been through, Tom has defeated all the odds," said his friend and former high school teammate, Steve Loerke. "If there was one word I'd use to describe him, it would be perseverance."

Brady needed all the resolve he could muster in his first playoff game, which was played against the Oakland Raiders on a day in which winds swirled and steadily falling snow covered the turf at Foxboro.

The climatic conditions threw a wet blanket over the teams' offenses, and at halftime Brady had completed only six passes for 74 yards, and the Pats trailed 7-0. Instead of slinking off to a corner of the locker room, however, Brady collected the offense around him and let them know that the second half would be different.

"He gathered the squad and told them that they could do better, and that he would do better," said Pats' safety Lawyer Milloy. "He's young, but he's a leader."

In the second half, Brady backed up his brave locker room words by passing for 238 yards and scrambling into the end zone for a touchdown that cut the deficit to 13-10 with 7:52 left to play. But he really showed his colors near the end of the fourth quarter, when he directed an eight-play drive that set up Adam Vinatieri's game-tying 45-yard field goal with only 27 seconds left in regulation.

In the overtime session, with the snow still falling and darkness descending around the flood-lit stadium, Brady completed six straight passes to move the ball down to the Raiders five yard line, perfectly positioning Vinatieri's 23-yard game-winning three-pointer.

"He never seems to get rattled," said an admiring Troy Brown, who was Brady's go-to wide receiver. "You never see him put his head down or get upset about making a bad throw. The way he behaves lets people know that he has confidence in what he's doing, and that, in turn, makes us believe that we can get it done."

Belichick, who had watched and suffered as the Patriots staggered through a 5-11 finish the year before, appreciated just how far the team had come in one season.

"I can't say enough about this group," said Belichick. "They will not quit. To pull our way back we had to make a lot of big plays. It can't get much closer than it did."

The win sent the Patriots to Pittsburgh for the AFC Conference Championship Game against the Steelers, who had compiled a conference-best 13-3 record. In a strange twist of fate, it was Brady who suffered an injury, and Bledsoe who rode to the rescue and led the Pats to a 24-17 come-from-behind win.

Belichick, faced with the choice of sticking with Bledsoe, who had been the Pats' starter since they had selected him with the No. 1 overall pick in the 1993 draft, or putting the ball back in Brady's hands for the upcoming Super Bowl game against the St. Louis Rams, decided to tie the team's fortunes to its first-year starter.

"To know, to really know that you're going to be starting the game, that's pretty exciting," said Brady, his eyes twinkling. "It's really a dream come true to be a quarterback and start a Super Bowl game. It's probably the highlight of my life, so far.

"From the time I got here, I've just been preparing myself for the opportunity to play," he continued. "Even when I wasn't playing during my first three years at Michigan, I was ready to go. The same thing happened here. I prepared myself as hard as I could, mentally and physically, watching and learning. And we've gone out this year and played pretty well."

Although Bledsoe was emotionally bleeding about being discarded, he handled the decision more gracefully than most people probably would have.

"It's not an accident that he's come in and played very, very well," said Bledsoe. "He has worked at it and, honestly, earned everything he's done this year. As hard as it was to stand there and watch someone else play my position, it was also very gratifying to see one of the truly good guys be rewarded for hard work and dedication. "

The Pats and their young quarterback came into Super Bowl XXXVI as the underdogs to a Rams team that had posted an NFL-best 14-2 record, which included a 24-17 win over the Pats in Week 10. The Rams had a potent offense, which featured most of the same players who had led St. Louis to a Super Bowl victory two years earlier, including a pair of former MVP Award-winners, quarterback Kurt Warner and running back Marshall Faulk.

But after Brady threw a short touchdown pass to wideout David Patten on an out-and-up route near the end of the second quarter, it was the New Englanders who went into the locker room with a 14-3 halftime lead. Brady had helped free his receiver with a pump fake that froze Rams' cornerback Dexter McCleon for a split second just as Patten made his cut; all the time that an NFL receiver needs to separate himself from his defender.

"A huge throw, because we didn't want to settle for a field goal there," said Patten. "He put the ball right where it had to be."

But Brady struggled to complete passes in the second half and the Pats' offense stalled, while the Rams came back and tied the score with 90 seconds left in regulation time. With the game on the line, however, Brady rose to the occasion and completed five of eight passes, enough to set up Vinatieri's game-winning field goal on the final play of the game.

"You can't say enough about that kid," said Patten. "He has a tremendous amount of confidence, and that allowed him to lead this team. Maybe he didn't have the greatest statistics today, but that doesn't matter. What does matter is that he knows how to win and motivate other players. My hat is off to him."

Brady, who had thrown for only 145 yards, didn't care about his numbers either.

"What's important is to play your best football when the game is on the line," said Brady, who was named the game's MVP. "We did this against Oakland; we did it at Pittsburgh; and we did it again tonight. We've got a whole team full of underdogs, but now we're the top dogs.

"When I replaced Drew, I was just hoping to get us some wins, and to be a better player at the end of the year than at the beginning," he continued. "Certainly, I'm better, and this is just the icing on what's become a pretty good cake. You dream about this kind of stuff, every player does, but it usually doesn't become reality. This is just amazing, but that's what this team is all about, and I'm just a little piece of the puzzle."

"It's been quite a year for Serra," said Pete Jensen, who was Brady's high school baseball coach. "Swann gets inducted into the Hall of Fame, Bonds hits 73 home runs, and now Tom Brady."

When Brady was asked what other people could learn from his dramatic rise from relative obscurity to Super Bowl MVP, his answer mirrored his own life and determined attitude.

"Don't let other people tell you what you're capable of," said Brady, who had just become the youngest quarterback ever to win a Super Bowl. "Just believe in yourself and keep plugging away and working hard to achieve what you set your mind to. It may not happen within your timetable but, eventually, you can get it done."

5 CLOSE DOESN'T CUT IT

Brady had risen from relative obscurity to Super Bowl MVP with incredible swiftness, and he was determined not to slide back toward the abyss of anonymity. He knew that the sports world was littered with players who had abandoned their work ethic after a season of glory, and then paid for their lack of effort with a season, or more, of mediocrity. Brady wasn't about to add his name to that list or take his new-found status for granted, not even after the Pats had expressed their belief in him by trading Drew Bledsoe to the Bills during the 2002 NFL draft.

"If you get to the point where you're complacent, there's always somebody else working hard who's ready to take your job," noted Brady, who wasn't about to allow himself to be sandbagged by a swollen ego or distracted by too many outside interests. "My biggest fear is being a one-hit wonder, so I'm not going to forget who I am or what got me here."

His work habits and commitment to excellence were appreciated by his teammates, who knew how easy it could be for a player, especially a young player who had just tasted his first season of success in the NFL, to lose his focus.

"He's been here at seven in the morning, throwing and running throughout the off-season," said Pats' linebacker Larry Izzo. "He works like he's still the sixth-round draft pick trying to make the team, not like he's the Super Bowl MVP. That's why he's become a leader of this team. He earned our respect by working as hard as he does."

When he wasn't exercising his body in preparation for the physical grind of the upcoming season, Brady could usually be found in the film room, where he'd spend five hours a day watching tapes of opposing defenses with his coaches, and then devising strategies to defeat those defenses. David Nugent, a defensive end who shared a condo with Brady, asked him how he could possibly spend five useful hours a day watching tape.

"He told me," said Nugent, 'When I come up to the line on Sundays, I'll know exactly what I'm facing and how to counteract it because of the time I'm putting in now. The key to being a winning quarterback is preparation.' I have a lot more respect for quarterbacks after rooming with Tom, because I realize how much they have to learn. It's not a position for the unintelligent."

All the work that Brady had put in during the off-season was on display at the outset of the 2002 season, as the Pats posted high-scoring wins over the Steelers, Jets and Kansas City Chiefs, whom they defeated in overtime. In those three games, Brady threw nine touchdown passes and only two interceptions. He started his run by throwing a trio of TD tosses against the Steelers and was named the AFC Offensive Player of the Week. He ended it by ripping the Kansas City secondary for four touchdown throws and 410 passing yards, a career high and the sixth-highest total in franchise history.

"He's just hit the tip of the iceberg on how good he can really be," said Izzo. "I mean, he still sees that there's a lot of things that he could do better, and just think of where he can go from here after having a great year, a Pro Bowl year. The sky's the limit, and I think he realizes that."

But the early season fireworks fizzled in their next game, a 21-14 loss in San Diego, as LaDainian Tomlinson ripped off huge chunks of yardage and tripped up the Pats with a pair of long touchdown runs.

"I don't think we played our best game," said Brady, who, ironically, had thrown for 355 yards, the third-highest total of his career at the time. "That's not an excuse. I think the important thing is that you take the good things, you learn from the bad things, and you move on."

The Pats moved on, but any learning that they might have absorbed wasn't immediately apparent, as they dropped their next three games. Brady's quality of play also took a nosedive, and he wound up throwing more interceptions than touchdown passes during the trio of losses.

The Pats finally stopped the slide with a 38-7 blowout win in Buffalo, as Brady put on a quarterback clinic, and was named the AFC Offensive Player of the Week for the second time in 2002. In completing 22 of 26 of his pass attempts, three of which went for touchdowns, Brady posted an almost-perfect 147.6 quarterback rating. Bledsoe had posted pretty good passing numbers, too, but he wasn't able to put points up on the scoreboard; and at the end of the game, quarterbacks are, mostly, judged by wins and losses.

The win over the Bills had evened the Pats record at 4-4 and given them a platform from which to make a second-half charge at the playoffs.

With Brady back on track, New England started their stretch run with a thrilling come-from-behind 33-31 victory at Chicago. The Bears thought they had locked the game away with a 31-19 lead and only 5:16 left to play, but Brady broke their backs by throwing for two late touchdowns, including the game-winner to David Patten, which came with only 21 ticks left on the clock.

They came into the final game of the season at Foxboro needing a win over Miami to keep their slim playoff hopes alive. But the Dolphins took it to the Pats and built up a 24-13 lead with less than five minutes left to play in regulation time. And then, just when all seemed lost, Brady began his ride to the rescue by throwing a TD pass to Troy Brown, followed by a two-point conversion toss to tight end Christian Fauria that cut their deficit to three points with less than three minutes to go. He continued his salvage mission with a drive that set up Adam Vinatieri's game-tying field goal, and then he completed it with a drive in OT that positioned Vinatieri's game-winning three-pointer.

The 27-24 win, Brady's fifth-straight OT victory, had upped the Pats record to 9-7, which tied them for first place in the division with the Dolphins and the Jets. But it was the Jets, based on the NFL's tiebreaker rules, who made it into the post-season, while the Dolphins and the Pats were on the outside looking in.

Brady had posted a fine follow-up season by throwing for a league-high 28 touchdown passes and only 14 interceptions, while finishing third in the AFC with 3,746 passing yards. But the stats didn't provide any consolation for Brady, who plays for championships, not for numbers.

"It was disappointing to come so close, and then not get the opportunity to defend our Super Bowl title," said Brady. "On the other hand, if we had played better and won another game, we would have been in the playoffs. We just didn't get it done."

6   MOVING UP THE LADDER

The Patriots started the 2003 season on the wrong foot when they went to Buffalo and were blown out by the Bills, 31-0. It was a sweet win for Drew Bledsoe, and safety Lawyer Milloy, who had been released a few days before the start of the season, after he'd anchored New England's secondary for seven seasons. But the loss left an especially sour taste in the mouth of Brady, who was picked off four times and sacked twice.

The Pats took a step back in the right direction the following week, however, by going on the road and defeating the Philadelphia Eagles, 31-10. It was also a personal bounce-back game for Brady, who passed for three touchdowns. It was the first time that Brady had shared a field with Donovan McNabb since McNabb had led Syracuse to a victory over Michigan in Brady's second college start.

The Pats also split their next two games, a win at home against the Jets, followed by a loss in Washington. With a quarter of the season gone, New England was sitting with a 2-2 record, and Brady, with seven interceptions and only five touchdown passes, was as responsible as anyone for the team's mediocre start.

Suddenly, though, the team jelled, Brady got hot, and the Patriots ran the table, winning all of their remaining twelve games, to finish the season with an NFL-best 14-2 record and the AFC East title.

They started their run with a hard-fought, 38-30, win over the Tennessee Titans, and there were a number of other games along the way when the streak was almost ended. The first near-loss occurred in Miami, two weeks after the Titans game, but Brady stepped up and saved the day by connecting on an 82-yard pass play with Troy Brown that gave the Pats a 19-13 overtime win.

Two weeks later, Brady led New England to a come-from-behind 30-16 win in Denver when he teamed up with wide receiver David Givens on a game-winning scoring strike with only 18 seconds left to play. The throw completed an exquisite game for Brady, who threw for 350 yards and three touchdowns, and was named the AFC Offensive Player of the Week.

Brady also rode to the rescue in Houston when, with 40 seconds remaining in the fourth quarter, he threw a short, game-tying touchdown pass to tight end Daniel Graham. The Pats then went on to beat the Texans in OT, which improved Brady's record in overtime games to a perfect 7-0.

New England finished their regular season run with a 31-0 blowout win over Buffalo, a mirror image of their opening day loss. It was also a stunning reversal from that first game for Brady, who passed for a season-high four touchdowns and was named the AFC Offensive Player of the Week for the second time in 2003.

Brady finished the season with another set of impressive stats and his second invitation in three years to the Pro Bowl, but, more importantly, the Patriots had made it back into post-season play and he was going to have the opportunity to try for a second Super Bowl ring.

New England started its playoff drive at Foxboro

with a rematch against the Titans, who were led by quarterback Steve McNair, the NFL's co-MVP in 2003. The second game was different from the first one in almost every way, beginning with the bone-chilling four-degree weather at kick-off. In addition to numbing the players, the cold also made the ball slick and hard to grip, so, unlike the first game, this one turned into a gritty defensive struggle.

With the teams knotted at 14-14 deep into the fourth quarter, Brady, who had thrown for the Pats' first score and set up the second with his passing, led New England on a short drive down to the Titans' 27-yard line. When the drive stalled, Vinatieri came into the game and split the uprights with a kick that sent New England into the AFC Championship game against Indianapolis.

"The ball was hard because of the cold," said Vinatieri, who had missed an earlier attempt, "but the nice thing about it was that I couldn't feel my feet."

Vinatieri also played a major role in the Patriots' win the following week, by kicking five field goals at Foxboro, as New England ended the Colts' season with a 24-14 win. Indianapolis had made it into the title game behind the passing of Peyton Manning, who had thrown seven touchdown passes in the team's playoff wins over Denver and Kansas City. But the New England defense, which had been superb throughout the season, stifled Manning, who had shared NFL MVP honors with McNair, and picked off four of his passes.

"This is the ultimate team defense, and this is the ultimate team," said cornerback Ty Law, who had intercepted Manning three times. "If we continue to play together, we feel as though we can beat anybody."

Although Brady hadn't been especially sharp or produced great stats, he had, once again, showed that he could somehow do enough to win a big game.

"Tom Brady is the greatest winner in football right now," said Law. "Maybe his numbers aren't eye-popping, but those other quarterbacks, with all their awards and stats, are sitting at home. I'll play with Tom any day."

The Patriots were matched against the Carolina Panthers in Super Bowl XXXVIII, which was played in Houston's Reliant Stadium. The game started out as a defensive struggle, with neither team able to move the ball or put points up on the scoreboard for most of the first half. But both offenses suddenly sprang to life, and generated a non-stop scoring spree that produced 24 points in the final three minutes before intermission.

New England struck first, but only after the defense had put them in the red zone by recovering a fumble at the Panthers' 20-yard line. Brady cashed in on the opportunity by throwing a short touchdown pass to wide receiver Deion Branch, who was tremendous throughout the game and led all receivers with 10 catches and 143 receiving yards.

After the following kickoff, the Panthers finally converted their initial offensive first down of the day, when their quarterback, Jake Delhomme, delivered a 13-yard pass to Ricky Proehl as the two-minute warning sounded. The play seemed to instantly energize the Panthers' moribund offense, as Delhomme went right back to the well and hooked up with Proehl for another first down. Then, from the Pats' 39-yard line, Delhomme spotted Steve Smith, his speedy wide receiver, streaking down the left sideline and delivered a beautifully thrown touch-down pass that evened the score at 7-7 with 1:07 left in the first half. The Panthers, who had been stymied for almost all of the first half, had suddenly solved the New England defense on a 95-yard scoring drive, the second-longest ever in a Super Bowl.

With time ticking down, Brady struck quickly, finding Branch on a 52-yard pass play that took the ball down to the Panthers' 14. Then, after connecting with David Givens on a nine-yard pass, he came right back to the wideout for a five-yard scoring pass that put the Pats back in front, 14-7.

The Panthers returned Vinatieri's short kick-off into New England territory at their 47-yard line, and with only 12 seconds left in the half. But that was all the time that was needed for Carolina running back Stephen Davis to rip off a 21-yard run off right tackle and set up John Kasay's 50-yard field goal that narrowed their half-time deficit to 14-10.

The sudden spurt of scoring at the end of the second quarter was followed by a scoreless third period. But, as the quarter was winding down, Brady led the Patriots on a long drive. The key play of the possession was a 33-yard pass to tight end Daniel Graham that put the ball on the Panthers' nine-yard line. Running back Antowain Smith completed the 71-yard drive with a short burst into the end zone at the 14:49 mark of the fourth quarter that increased New England's advantage to 21-10.

Trailing by two scores, and with the ticking clock becoming a factor, the Panthers went to their no-huddle offense in an attempt to conserve time. The shift in tac-tics turned the Panthers' offense on as if it was a light-switch, and they were able to dissect a defense that had kept them contained for most of the game. Delhomme led the Panthers down to the Patriots' 33-yard line with three quick pass plays, then, with the Pats thinking pass, he handed the ball off to running back DeShaun Foster, who took it to the house. Although their attempt at a two-point conversion failed, Foster's touchdown run had cut New England's lead to 21-16 with 12:32 left to play.

Trying to widen their lead, the Pats' offense shifted into a higher gear on their next possession, as Brady led them on a 64-yard drive down to the Carolina nine-yard line. But just when they seemed on the brink of stretching their lead, Brady was picked off and the Panthers took over deep in their own territory with 7:38 left on the clock.

Carolina was quick to cash in on the opportunity, as Delhomme and Muhammad teamed up on an 85-yard touchdown connection, the longest play from scrimmage in Super Bowl history. Although the Panthers missed another chance at a two-point conversion, they had taken a 22-21 lead with 6:53 left to play.

Faced with their first scoring deficit in three months, the Pats struck quickly, with Brady eating up a large chunk of the field with two passes to Givens, the second of which moved the ball down to the Carolina three. After a Smith run down to the one, Brady faked a hand-off and then threw a touchdown to Vrabel, who had been brought in on the play as an extra tight end.

"Going into the game, that was our lead play-action pass play," said Charlie Weis. "A few days before the Super Bowl, I had told Vrabel, 'When we get down there we're going to call that play, and you're going to score a touchdown.'"

The Pats also added a two-point conversion, which gave them a 29-22 lead with 2:51 left to play. But that was more than enough time for Delhomme to lead the Panthers down the field and tie up the game with a 12-yard pass to Proehl.

With overtime staring both teams in the face, Kasay flubbed the kick-off, allowing New England to put the ball in play from their 40-yard line with only 1:08 left in regulation time.

"That was critical," said Weis. "That made the play-calling a lot easier. Now, instead of having to go 40 or 50 yards, we only had to go 30 yards to be within Adam's range."

But the Pats' offense still had to go out and execute the playbook and, as they came into the huddle, Brady delivered a simple message to his teammates.

"Let's get this done," he told them, and then, as the tension mounted and the clock hands moved toward triple zero, he completed four passes, the last of which was a 17-yarder down to Branch at the Carolina 23 with 0:09 left to play.

Then, with the crowd and the players on each sideline up on their feet, Vinatieri, who had missed an earlier field goal attempt and had had another one blocked, trotted on to the field and calmly sent a 41-yard kick sailing through the uprights to give New England their second Super Bowl win in three years.

"We always have confidence that we can get it done, but it's unbelievable to do it the way we did it," said

Brady, who was selected as the Super Bowl MVP, again, after completing a Super Bowl-record 32 passes for 345 yards and three touchdowns.

"Tom's moving up the ladder of the league's best quarterbacks," said Belichick. "He deserves to be mentioned with all the best quarterbacks. Tom's a winner. He does that as well as anybody, and much better than almost anyone."

7 THREE OUT OF FOUR

The Patriots started the 2004 season with six straight victories, which upped their consecutive-game winning streak to 21, a new NFL record. The previous record, 16 straight, was an achievement that had been reached by several teams.

The winning came to a decisive end in Pittsburgh, however, when the Steelers defeated the Patriots on Halloween, 34-20. The goblins certainly seemed to get to Brady, who coughed up a fumble and threw a pair of interceptions.

But the Patriots bounced right back and won eight of their final nine games, to finish the season at 14-2 for the second successive year and capture the AFC East title for the third time in Brady's four seasons as the team's starter.

Brady, who had been voted an offensive captain by his teammates in 2004, had produced another superior season, finishing it with 3,692 passing yards, 28 touchdown passes (which tied his career-high), 14 interceptions—six of which came in New England's only two losses—and a career-high 92.6 quarterback rating. But Brady had lots of help, including a fine receiving corps, a solid offensive line, and running back Corey Dillon, who had signed with New England after having spent seven seasons with the Cincinnati Bengals, and proceeded to rack up 1,635 rushing yards and 13 touchdowns.

The defensive unit, which allowed the second-fewest points in the league in 2004, was also a tower of strength. The defense was as adept at stopping the run as it was at defending the pass. Strong safety Rodney Harrison, who had been brought in as a free agent the previous year to replace Lawyer Milloy, totaled 138 tackles, to top all NFL defensive backs for the second straight year.

The Patriots began the post-season part of their Super Bowl defense by again hosting Indianapolis, who had led the NFL in scoring by a vast margin. Peyton Manning, who was named the league MVP again, had crafted an incredible year, passing for an NFL-record 49 touchdowns, one more than Dan Marino had thrown for the Dolphins in 1984. He'd continued his amazing aerial act in Indianapolis' opening round playoff game by lighting up the Broncos with four more touchdown passes, and the Colts came into Foxboro under a full head of steam after defeating Denver, 49-24.

"You're not going to stop them," said Denver coach Mike Shanahan. "You just have to try to slow them down. And the only way to slow them down is to keep them off the field."

But New England's defense stopped the Colts in their tracks, paving the way for a 20-3 Patriots' win. Brady, meanwhile, threw for one score and ran for another, his second career post-season touchdown, and Dillon ate up clock time by rushing for 144 yards.

"He's incredible," said tight end Christian Fauria, speaking about Brady. "He's never yet let us down."

The Patriots had to travel to Heinz Field to play the AFC Championship Game in Pittsburgh, where their 21-

game winning streak had been brought to an end three months earlier. The Steelers had gone on to post an NFL-best 15-1 record during the regular season, and then they beat the Jets in a divisional playoff game. Offensively, the Steelers were led by a grinding running game and by quarterback Ben Roethlisberger, who had piloted Pittsburgh to 13 straight wins, and was named the NFL Offensive Rookie of the Year. On the other side of the line of scrimmage, the Steelers had created a modern day version of their legendary Steel Curtain defense, and it had been the stingiest team in the NFL, allowing only 15.6 points per game.

But it was the New England defense that set the tone by picking off Roethlisberger's first pass. Brady then went right at the Steelers' defense, and opened the scoring with a 60-yard touchdown strike to Deion Branch, the longest pass completion in Patriots' history. After Brady had led New England on two additional first-half scoring drives, which upped their lead to 17-3, the Steelers mounted a counter-attack and moved the ball into the shadow of the Pats' end zone. But when Roethlisberger tried to throw for the Steelers first touchdown, Rodney Harrison stepped in front of his pass, and turned it into an 87-yard touchdown return that opened the Patriots lead to 24-3 at halftime.

"It's amazing to watch," said Pats' linebacker Ted Johnson, referring to Brady's errorless performance. "There are other outstanding quarterbacks, but he just has an uncanny ability to rise up at the most critical times. And he does it time after time."

After the intermission, Brady, who had spent the night before the game sick in bed with the flu, flawlessly guided the Patriots to 17 second-half points and a 41-24 victory. After the game, when some reporters tried to make too much of his illness, Brady got annoyed with them.

"It wasn't a big deal, and I don't want it to take away from what everyone else on the team has accomplished" he explained. "Everyone else plays with toughness and never complains. Guys in our locker room have played with broken bones."

Brady also became a bit testy when he was asked what he thought about his 8-0 record in playoff games.

"There are a bunch of guys in this locker room who are 8-0, and I'm just one of them," said Brady. "But we're all proud to be going back to the Super Bowl for a second year in a row."

The day after the AFC Championship game ended, Brady was in the film room, watching tape of the Philadelphia Eagles, New England's opponent in Super Bowl XXXIX. Typically, he would watch tape until 11:00 at night and be in the weight room the following morning at 6:30, before any of his teammates had even finished their breakfast.

"The rest of us were still eating scrambled eggs," noted Rodney Harrison. "Tom is always preparing, always working to gain that extra edge."

For Brady, putting in all the work that he does allows him to go into games with confidence, knowing that he, with a great deal of help from his coaches, has solved the riddle of opposing defenses and knows how to exploit their weaknesses.

"There's no reason to be worried," said Brady, who was so relaxed before Super Bowl XXXVI that he had fallen asleep in the locker room on game day. "I feel like I'm going into the test with all the answers."

Of course, there are things in life that can't be prepared for, as Brady was reminded of when his 94-year-old grandmother, Margaret Brady, passed away on the Wednesday night before the Super Bowl.

"She had been ill for quite some time, but things suddenly took a turn for the worse," said Brady. "Hopefully, I can live to be 94 and have a full life like she did."

Although Brady was as prepared as he could be when the Patriots ran on to the floodlit field of Jacksonville's Alltel Stadium, he knew that he was going up against the NFC's top-rated defensive unit and a secondary that was sending three of its four members to the Pro Bowl.

Brady would have liked to get the jump on that formidable defense by putting points on the scoreboard quickly, but it was the Eagles who struck first, as Donovan McNabb capped a long second quarter drive with a six-yard touchdown pass to tight end L.J. Smith.

The New England offense, which had been stymied throughout the first half, finally started to move, but Brady and running back Kevin Faulk fumbled an exchange and the Eagles recovered the ball on their four-yard line. The next time the Patriots got their hands on the ball, however, Brady led them on another drive deep into Philadelphia territory. With the ball on the Eagles' four, Brady back-pedaled and, after looking left and checking off his two primary receivers, found David Givens in the right corner of the end zone for the game-tying touchdown pass, 70 seconds before halftime.

Brady went right to work in the second half, teaming with Branch on three big passing plays, and then lofting a two-yard touchdown pass to Mike Vrabel that put the Patriots ahead, 14-7. But McNabb answered back by leading the Eagles on a 10-play, 74-yard drive that he capped with a 10-yard scoring pass to running back Brian Westbrook, tying the score at 14-14 with 3:35 left in the third quarter.

The Pats' offense, which had been so docile for most of the first half, roared right back into action on their next possession, with Brady leading them on a 69-yard scoring drive that ended with Corey Dillon bursting into the end zone early in the fourth quarter. After a Philadelphia punt, Brady led the Patriots down the field again and, when the drive stalled deep in Eagles' territory, Adam Vinatieri kicked a 22-yard field goal, which upped their lead to 24-14 with 8:40 left to play.

"Hands down, he's the best we've faced," said Eagles' strong safety Mike Lewis. "I don't know another quarterback in the league who plays at his level."

The Eagles later narrowed the Patriots' lead to 24-21 on a McNabb touchdown pass with 1:48 left in the game. But that was as close as Philadelphia came, because Rodney Harrison picked off McNabb's last desperate pass with 10 seconds left, securing New England's third Super Bowl victory in the previous four years.

The only franchises with more Super Bowl wins are the San Francisco 49ers and the Dallas Cowboys, who have won it five times each, and the Pittsburgh Steelers, who have hoisted the Vince Lombardi Trophy four times. The Cowboys, though, are the only other team that has been able to win three Super Bowls in a four-year span. But when the talk turned to the word 'dynasty,' the Patriots' seemed totally disinterested.

"We started at the bottom of the mountain with everyone else and we're happy to get to the top," said Belichick, who had raised his post-season coaching mark to 10-1, one better than the record of Vince Lombardi, who coached the Green Bay Packers to five NFL titles in the 1960s, the last two of which were in Super Bowls I and II. "I'll leave the historical perspectives to everyone else."

Brady, whose ninth consecutive playoff win had tied the NFL record set by the former Green Bay quarterback, Bart Starr, was equally unconcerned with discussions about dynasties.

"If you guys in the media say we're a great team, then we accept the compliment," said Brady. "But we just love playing football. It's as simple as that. We love to the play the game, and we play it like it's supposed to be played—as a team."

8   DOWN IN DENVER

Just how much the Patriots' success had been dependent upon the contributions of the entire team would become apparent throughout the trying 2005 season.

With their three Super Bowl wins in four years, the Patriots had, without question, proven that they were a superior franchise. The accomplishments of the players however, were not merely the end results of their own collective efforts. Their performances on the field were also an extension and reflection of the excellence of the Patriots' entire organization, including owner Robert Kraft; president Jonathan Kraft; vice president-player personnel Scott Pioli and the other front office personnel, and Bill Belichick and his coaching crew.

But the staff that Belichick had assembled when he arrived as New England's head coach in 1999 began to fracture even before the team was finished celebrating its latest Super Bowl win. Defensive coordinator Romeo Crennel stepped away to accept the head coaching job with the Cleveland Browns, and his offensive counterpart, Charlie Weis, who had worked very closely with Brady, was hired as the head coach at Notre Dame.

The team also had to suffer through a spate of serious injuries to key players, including linebackers Tedy Bruschi and Ted Johnson, safety Rodney Harrison, and running backs Corey Dillon and Kevin Faulk. As a result of all the changes and injuries, the Patriots got off to a shaky start in 2005, and made it to the halfway point of the season with only a 4-4 record.

One of their four losses came at the hands of the San Diego Chargers, who had come into Foxboro and ended the Patriots' 21-game home winning streak with a 41-17 blowout. The 41 points were the most scored against New England in nearly seven seasons.

Even after the Chargers had built up a 31-17 fourth-quarter lead, Brady's reputation as a game-changer had caused LaDainian Tomlinson, San Diego's All-Pro running back, to hold his breath until the Chargers had salted away the game with a nine minute drive.

"We needed that drive because you can't give the ball back to Brady," said Tomlinson, who had nailed New England for 134 rushing yards and two touchdowns. "You have to keep it away from him, because he's able to make so many things happen."

Brady had, in fact, continued to make good things happen despite the absence of so many injured players, and he had been the main reason that the Patriots had been able to split the first eight games of the season. By the second half of the season, some of the sidelined players had retuned, and the Patriots were able to finish their schedule with a 10-6 record and capture their third successive AFC East title.

Brady, meanwhile, had turned in an exceptional season, which included a career-high and league-leading 4,110 passing yards, and four game-winning fourth-quarter drives.

"I think I've grown into the role the coaches have given me," said Brady, who was named to the NFL's All-

Pro team for the first time. "I just feel good out there and do whatever I can to help the team win."

Through the bad times and the good times, Brady had stood tall as one of the team's few constants, and when they needed him most, he had, arguably, delivered his finest season to date.

"Tom has been a great leader for this football team this year and every year," said Belichick. "He had an outstanding season, but he also brings so much to our team with his preparation, his work ethic, his toughness and his ability to lead our offense and our team. I'm very glad that he's our quarterback."

With the struggle of the regular season in their rearview mirror, the Patriots were looking forward to the playoffs and hoping to become the first team in NFL history to win three straight Super Bowl titles.

The Patriots began their post-season journey with a 28-3 wild-card victory over the Jacksonville Jaguars. Although the final score might suggest otherwise, the first half of the game was a tense, defensive struggle, with both offenses struggling to gain traction and put points on the board.

Although the Jags scored first, they weren't able to move the ball with any consistency against the relentless New England defense, which racked up six sacks against Jacksonville quarterback Byron Leftwich. Willie McGinest registered 4.5 of those sacks, a new post-season single-game record, and he also became the NFL's all-time post-season career sack leader with 16.

Brady, meanwhile, began to solve the Jag's defense so deftly that he wound up throwing a trio of touchdown passes, one each to Troy Brown, David Givens, and tight end Ben Watson, who took a short pass and turned it into a spectacular 63-yard score. For Givens, the score marked the sixth straight playoff game in which he had caught a touchdown pass.

"Tom Brady just seems to have a knack for knowing what to do in every situation," said Reggie Hayward, a Jacksonville defensive end. "He knows how to handle whatever defenses are called against them, and he knows when to check off a play and call an audible. He just knows the game."

Six plays after Watson's tackle-breaking run, Asante Samuel picked off a Leftwich pass at the New England 27-yard line and turned the interception into a 73-yard, game-clinching touchdown return.

The win was the Patriots' 10th straight post-season victory, an NFL record, but even before they left Foxboro, they were already thinking about the next steps on the path to the Super Bowl.

"It's a great accomplishment," noted McGinest. "We're not downplaying it, but they're not passing out any trophies tonight. We've got a long way to go."

But New England's dream of an unprecedented third straight Super Bowl championship died in Denver, where they were beaten by the Broncos, 27-13. At least, that's what the scoreboard said, but the reality of the game was that the Patriots beat themselves. After winning 10 straight playoff games with only six turnovers, New England, with three fumbles and two interceptions, turned the ball over to Denver five times. In fact, all but three of Denver's points were the result of the Patriots' miscues.

The most crushing turnover occurred in the third quarter, as the Patriots, who were down by only 10-6, seemed poised to take the lead. With the ball at Denver's five-yard line, Brady threw a pass to Troy Brown, who was at the goal line. But Champ Bailey, the Broncos' All-Pro cornerback, closed quickly, made the pick, and returned it all the way down to New England's one-yard line. It was the longest non-scoring interception return in NFL playoff history. On the next play, running back Mike Anderson took the ball into the end zone. Instead of possibly trailing 13-10, Denver had a 17-6 lead.

"I gave Champ the game ball, so that tells you what I thought about that play," said Denver coach Mike Shanahan. "That was the turning point in the game, obviously."

Fittingly, New England's final offensive play of the game was a Brady pass that was picked off by Denver safety John Lynch.

The team that had rarely beaten itself, and never in the post-season, had all at once become sloppier than anyone could have imagined.

"When you lose, you want to at least go down fighting," said Brady. "You want to go down playing your best, but we didn't do that. We made it easy for them."

9   WAIT UNTIL NEXT YEAR

The pain from the loss to the Broncos stayed with the Patriots' players throughout the off-season, like a dull ache burrowed in the back of one's brain. What hurt so much was not the final score, but the knowledge that they had failed to perform up to their abilities, and that they had played so poorly in such a big game.

"Realistically, we know that we're not going to win every game or capture every Super Bowl," acknowledged Brady. "But there's a difference between being beaten and beating yourself. We could live with being beaten, but beating yourself is a lot harder to deal with."

If there was a plus side to the loss it was that the players were able to use it to help fuel their motivation for the 2006 season. But some of the players who had played especially important roles on the team were no longer there. Adam Vinatieri, who had kicked so many game-winning field goals for New England, signed with the Indianapolis Colts. And Deion Branch, Brady's favorite receiver and their only consistent downfield threat was traded to the Seattle Seahawks. Although Vinatieri was capably replaced by rookie Stephen Gostkowski, the Patriots' passing game didn't come close to finding a suitable replacement for Branch.

Even without Branch, the Patriots were able to begin the 2006 season with a bang, winning six of their first seven games, and Brady, looking as sharp as he ever had, led the way with 14 touchdown passes. Their only defeat in that span came at the hands of Denver, who dropped into Foxboro and followed up their playoff win from the previous season with a 17-7 victory. Although Brady filled the air with footballs, completing 31 of his 55 pass attempts for 320 yards, only one of his passes counted on the scoreboard.

Their second loss occurred in Week 8, when the Colts came to town and took down the Patriots, 27-20. Indianapolis' defense, usually their weak link, harried Brady into four interceptions, which equaled the total he had thrown in the season's first seven games.

At the halfway point of their schedule, the Patriots' record read 6-2, which put them on the road toward another playoff run. They did hit a slight speed bump the following week, when the Jets landed in Foxboro and went back home with a 17-14 win. For the Jets, it was payback for the Patriots' 24-17 win in Week 2 at Giants Stadium. But New England went right back to their winning ways, and closed out the regular season the same way they had started it, by taking six of their final seven games.

After finishing the regular season with a 12-4 record, which put them in their accustomed spot at the top of the AFC East standings, the Patriots were ready to focus all their attention on the playoffs.

Their opening round opponent was the Jets, an AFC East division rival, with whom they had split two games during the regular season. The Jets had made it into the playoffs as a wild-card team with only a 10-6 record, but they came into Gillette Stadium and gave the hometown Patriots all that they could handle.

Brady had helped get New England off to a quick lead by engineering a touchdown drive on the game's opening possession. Although the drive was fueled mainly by the passing game, Corey Dillon finished it off with a 10-yard run around the right side, striding into the end zone without a Jets' player having laid a hand on him. Later in the quarter, however, Dillon coughed up the ball at the Patriots' 14, and the Jets recovered his fumble and converted the turnover into a field goal, which cut New England's lead to 7-3. The Jets struck again in the second quarter when quarterback Chad Pennington hooked up with wide receiver Jericho Cotchery on a 77-yard pass-and-run play that gave the visitors a 10-7 lead. New England answered right back on their next possession, though, tying the game on Stephen Gostkowski's first post-season field goal. The teams stayed tied until just before halftime, and then, with only 14 seconds left until intermission and no time outs remaining, a Brady pass found Daniel Graham in the back of the end zone and the Patriots went into the locker room with a 17-10 lead.

The teams continued to battle back and forth into the fourth quarter, until the Patriots tallied two touchdowns and put the game out of reach. The first score came on Brady's second short TD toss of the day, which widened their lead to 30-16, and the second one was a 36-yard interception return by Asante Samuel, which closed out the scoring.

The Patriots had to fly to the West Coast for their next step on the playoff ladder, where their reward for beating the Jets was a showdown against the San Diego Chargers, who had finished the regular season with an

NFL-best 14-2 record. The Bolts, who had led the league in scoring, were widely considered to be the most talented team in the tournament, and were favored to go all the way and win their first Super Bowl.

At the top of the Chargers' talent tree was LaDainian Tomlinson, who had been named the NFL MVP after leading the league in scoring. But the group of gifted teammates surrounding LT was so strong that he was only one of the nine Bolts who had been selected to play in the 2007 Pro Bowl Game.

The Patriots, though, had played against and beaten other talented teams on their way to three Super Bowl titles, so they weren't about to be intimidated by the prospect of playing against the Bolts, or any other team.

As it turned out, Tomlinson, who totaled 187 yards, scored a pair of touchdowns and set up a third one with a 58-yard pass reception, did everything that he could do to dominate the Patriots' defense and lead the Chargers to the next step in their title hunt. Brady, who threw three interceptions in a post-season game for the first time in his career, didn't rise to the expectations that he had created by his performances in previous playoff games. Not, at least, until the final minutes of the fourth quarter, when the Patriots trailed the Bolts 21-13, and looked as though they were headed for an early vacation.

The comeback actually started right after the darkest moment of the day for the Patriots, when Morton McRee picked off a Brady pass and turned up field. During his return, however, Troy Brown stripped the ball away, and it was recovered at the Bolts' 32-yard line by Patriots' wide receiver Reche Caldwell, a former

Charger, who had signed with New England after the 2005 season.

Brady reacted to the sudden change of fortune by quickly leading the Patriots to a first down at the four. Then, he took the snap, faked a handoff to Corey Dillon, which froze the San Diego secondary, and then lofted a touchdown pass to Caldwell, who was all alone in the end zone. The Pats added a two-point conversion on a Kevin Faulk run, and the score was tied 21-21 with 4:36 left in regulation time.

The Bolts fielded the kickoff and had a golden opportunity to put points up on the scoreboard and run the clock out. But New England's defense came up big by causing a three-and-out, forcing the Chargers to punt the ball away.

With 3:30 left to play, Brady began New England's final drive of the day by completing a 19-yard pass to Graham, out to their own 34. After a couple of incomplete passes put the Patriots in the position of having to make a first down or punt the ball back to the Bolts, Brady made the play of the day with a 49-yard completion to Caldwell, who was racing down the right sideline.

When the drive stalled at the six, Gostkowski came out with 1:10 left in the game and calmly split the uprights with a 31-yard field goal that gave the Patriots a 24-21 lead; the first time they had been in front since they had led 3-0.

The Bolts had one more chance to prolong their season but, after Philip Rivers had passed the Chargers down to New England's 26-yard line, Nate Kaeding, one of their nine Pro Bowl players, was short on his 54-yard field goal try, and the Patriots left Qualcomm Stadium with another improbable playoff victory.

The comeback marked the sixth time in 13 playoff games that Brady had led the Patriots to a victory following a fourth-quarter tie or deficit. The win was also a perfect example of the fact that successful teams win games with contributions from a large cast of characters, including special teams players, and not simply from one star performer. It was also an instance, and not the first one, of Brady being better than his statistics and finding a way to let go of his mistakes and lead his team to victory when the game was on the line. The game also pointed out, and not for the first time, how much the defensive unit was needed; first, to limit the damage while Brady struggled, and, then, to hold off one last charge.

"Since I came here, I've been telling anyone who will listen that I don't accomplish anything by myself," said Brady. "The popular perception is that quarterbacks win and lose games by themselves. The fact is, we win and lose as a team."

The win sent New England to Indianapolis for the AFC Championship Game against the Colts and Peyton Manning, their perennial Pro Bowl quarterback. Manning had already amassed an amazing pile of passing records, but he would have been willing to trade every one of his records for any one of Brady's three Super Bowl wins.

The Patriots had done as much as any team to block the Colts' path to a championship, having knocked them off in two previous post-season meetings since Brady had come on the scene. And, for the first half of the game, it looked as though it was going to be more of the same, as the Patriots carried a 21-6 lead into the locker room at the RCA Dome.

The Colts, though, came roaring back in the second half and, with 5:31 to play, Vinatieri kicked a 28-yard field goal that knotted the game at 31-31. New England quickly regained the lead, however, as a 41-yard kickoff return by Ellis Hobbs set them up at their own 46-yard line. From there, Brady connected on a 25-yard pass to Daniel Graham and, when the drive stalled, Gostkowski split the uprights to give the Patriots a 34-31 lead with 3:49 left on the clock.

This time, though, the defense did not hold, as they had in the Chargers game and countless other games, and Manning led the Colts on an 80-yard touchdown drive that put them in the lead, 38-34 with 1:17 left to play. And this time, the Comeback Kid didn't have any rabbits to pull out of his hat. Instead, the game ended as the previous year's playoff loss to Denver had, with Brady throwing an interception.

"It's always sour when it ends," said Brady. "The competitive part of you always wants it to end at the Super Bowl. But we'll come back next year and try to do it better."

10   THE ROAD AHEAD

In his first six seasons as New England's starting quarterback, Brady has already put himself on the road to the Pro Football Hall of Fame. Brady is the only quarterback in NFL history to win three Super Bowl rings before his 28th birthday, and he is only the fourth quarterback to lead his team to three or more Super Bowl wins in a career. The other three who did it—Terry Bradshaw and Joe Montana, who won four titles each, and Troy Aikman, who won three Super Bowl championships—are all enshrined in the Hall of Fame.

His .762 career winning percentage (80-25) ranks first among all quarterbacks in the Super Bowl era, and he's shown a remarkable ability to pull victory out of the jaws of defeat by leading the Patriots to 23 game-winning drives after they were tied or behind in the fourth quarter.

Although Brady bowed out of the playoff picture in the past two seasons earlier than he would have liked or had become accustomed to, his 12-2 record and .857 winning percentage in post-season play is still the best of any quarterback in history, except for Bart Starr, who posted a 9-1 record and a .900 winning percentage.

Brady is sometimes compared to Montana, who was his boyhood sports idol, because Brady, like Montana, is known for maintaining his cool when the stakes and the heat are raised, and for winning multiple Super Bowls.

Even Bill Walsh, the Hall of Fame coach, who drafted and coached Montana, sees a similarity.

"He's as close to Joe as anyone I've ever seen," said Walsh. "Joe was unique, but I certainly see echoes of him in Tom."

Montana has also expressed his admiration for Brady's ability and composure.

"I just like watching him play, and seeing how he carries himself," said the man with the *Joe Cool* nickname. "He's always in control, and always doing the right thing. I think he's in a position to win a lot more championships, but it won't get easier. He'll find there is no end to the expectations."

Brady, meanwhile, deflects the praise and comparisons, and the talk about his place in football history.

"I'm very flattered, but I don't think I'm on that level; I'm still trying to get better," said Brady. "But what a great thing that would be, to play like one of the best quarterbacks of all time. But, I think I'm a long ways from that. I hope those comparisons are still around at the end of my career."

In the immediate future, Brady is looking forward to competing for a fourth Super Bowl title in 2007, and working with the talented collection of veteran receivers whom the Patriots signed after the end of the 2006 season; a group that includes Randy Moss, Donte Stallworth, and Wes Walker. But Brady knows that nothing in the NFL—or in life—is a given, and that the results will, in large part, depend upon how much work each member of the team is willing to put in.

"Talk is cheap, but if we all work as hard as we should, then it could be exciting," said Brady. "Still, the only thing that counts is when we go out there and we see what we're made of."

Brady, who is also looking forward to becoming a father for the first time around the start of the 2007 season, also has a life outside of football and is as committed and unselfish off the field as he is on it. After the end of the 2006 season, he traveled to Africa on behalf of ONE: The Campaign to Make Poverty History (www.one.org), and was deeply impressed by what he saw and what needs to be done.

"This was my first trip to Africa, and it was an eye-opener," said Brady. "I saw the best and brightest of the human spirit in the face of poverty that most of us just can't comprehend. I've learned that we as Americans, living in the greatest country in the world, can save innocent lives ravaged by AIDS with something as small as a pill that costs 25 cents. When you see what can be done, it's impossible not to be driven to do more—the needs are still so overwhelming. This won't be my last visit to Africa, and I hope to pass along what I've learned and seen to others."

TOM BRADY

Born: August 3, 1977, in San Mateo, California
Height: 6-4   Weight: 225
College: Michigan   Round drafted: Sixth   NFL Seasons: 7

CAREER STATS

Att.	Comp.	Pct.	Yards	TD	Int.	QB Rating
3,064	1,896	61.9	21,564	147	78	88.4

LADAINIAN TOMLINSON

Born: June 23, 1977, in Rosebud, Texas
Height: 5-10 **Weight:** 221
College: TCU **Round drafted:** First **NFL Seasons:** 6

CAREER STATS

	Rushing					Receiving		
Att.	Yards	Avg.	TD		No.	Yards	Avg.	TD
2,050	9,176	4.5	100		398	2,900	7.3	11

74

1 FINDING A ROLE MODEL

LaDainian Tomlinson was born June 23, 1979, in Rosebud, a tiny town, which is located in the eastern portion of Central Texas, 35 miles south of Waco, where Tomlinson would later move to and play his high school football.

For the first seven years of his life, Tomlinson and his father, Oliver, enjoyed a very strong relationship. During those good times, Tomlinson liked nothing better than to spend Saturdays watching college football games with his father, and then gathering in front of the television again on Sundays to watch the Dallas Cowboys.

"When I was a little kid, five, six years old, we used to watch the Cowboys every Sunday that they were on," recalled Tomlinson, whose favorite players were Dallas running backs Tony Dorsett and, after TD had retired, Emmitt Smith, as well as the Chicago Bears' great, Walter Payton. "I used to tell my mom, 'I'm going to be in the NFL some day.' I don't think she believed me, but she just said, 'Sure, baby, I know you are.'"

"They just loved those Cowboys," recalled Tomlinson's mother, Loreane Chappell, who goes by her maiden name. "They would just sprawl out on the living room floor, as happy as could be."

Tomlinson didn't just watch the games, as most children do when they're four years old; he studied all the action and seemed to absorb everything he saw.

"It was really remarkable," recalled his mother. "He knew all the players and their numbers. He could tell us what this one did, who kicked a field goal, and anything else about the game. He was amazing."

In 1986, however, when Tomlinson was only seven years old, his father and mother divorced. It was a wrenching blow for Tomlinson and his younger brother and older sister. But the situation was made even worse because Oliver Tomlinson, essentially, abandoned his family and left the entire burden of financial and emotional support of their three children on their mother.

LT's mother stepped right up and supported the family by working two jobs. She also gave the children the emotional support and guidance that they needed to go out into the world and hold their heads high.

"She taught me how to be a man, and that nothing ever gets handed to you," said Tomlinson, in explaining how his mother stressed the values of hard work and self-reliance. "She let us know that if we wanted to achieve our goals that we had to be prepared to go out and strive as hard as we could."

Although Oliver withdrew from his young son's life, all the hours that the two had spent together watching football games instilled a love of the sport in Tomlinson. The feelings went so deep, in fact, that LT slept with a football in his arms every night until he was in high school.

"That ball would lie in his arms like a girlfriend," recalled Tomlinson's younger brother LaVar. "And I can never remember it being on the floor."

When he was nine years old, LT joined a Pee Wee league football team. Even though he knew that his mother might not be thrilled with him playing such a rough game, he knew he could count on her support.

"A lot of parents don't want their children playing football at that young an age, which I understand," said Tomlinson. "But she knew how much I loved it and she stood by me. I didn't really have a father I could go to for advice, which my mother realized, so she played that role, too."

In what turned out to be a preview of things to come, Tomlinson ran for a touchdown the very first time he touched the ball in a Pee Wee league game.

"He always loved to play sports," said his mother. "He's just a natural athlete."

After he scored one of his many touchdowns, Tomlinson did an end zone dance, just like he had seen players do on television. The referee walked over to him and told him to knock it off.

"Son, you can't do that until you're in the NFL," said the referee, who, of course, had no idea that he was actually talking to a future pro star. That mild scolding motivated Tomlinson to begin simply flipping the ball to the referee after each score, without any dance or other showoff gestures. It's a tradition that he's continued to follow throughout his fabled career.

"Even when he was a child, he was always giving a lot of thought to different things," said his mom. "It seems as if he's had an adult mind all his life."

When LT was in the seventh grade, he received the biggest thrill of his young life when he got to meet Emmitt Smith at Smith's summer football camp. Tomlinson had begged his mom to come up with the $200 so that he could learn how to be a running back from one of the best. She agreed to chip in, but only if he raised some of the money himself by mowing neighborhood lawns.

Smith, who broke in with the Cowboys in 1990, led the league in rushing four times and was the NFL MVP in 1993, while helping the Cowboys corral three Super Bowl titles. During his 15 seasons in the league, the last two of which he played for the Arizona Cardinals, Smith scored 174 touchdowns and went on to become the NFL's all-time career leader in rushing yards, with 18,355, breaking the record that had been set by Walter Payton.

During one drill, Smith handed the ball off to Tomlinson, and at that moment LT thought that life couldn't get very much better.

"I'll always remember Emmitt from when I was growing up, and he was playing for the Cowboys," said Tomlinson, after Smith had announced his retirement. "It wasn't just his running that caught my attention, but all the things he did for the organization, and the way he handled himself. He was my role model."

When Tomlinson signed up for the football team at Waco University High School in his sophomore year, he hoped to be a running back. But the team's head coach, Leroy Coleman, played him at linebacker. Although Tomlinson wanted to play tailback, he was happy to be a part of the team, and didn't complain about the decision to play him on defense. The following year, Coleman switched LT to fullback, making him the lead blocker for a talented senior running back, Lawrence Pullen, who is currently playing wide receiver for Omaha in the United Indoor Football League.

"That's the way I've always done things here," said Coleman. "You earn your stripes by blocking for an upperclassman, then you get the chance to run the ball. No one gets to cut the line."

During the off-season between his junior and senior years, Tomlinson worked out extremely hard, because he knew that he had only that one season to impress college coaches and, hopefully, move closer to his dream of becoming an NFL running back.

"That was one of my motivating factors; to work hard in the off-season so that I'd play well enough to earn a college scholarship," said Tomlinson. "I never wanted to have to look back and know that I didn't give it everything I had."

Before the start of his senior year, however, Tomlinson received a jolt when his mother told him that the family needed to move to Dallas, so that she could get a better job. He had waited two years for the opportunity to play tailback, and he didn't want to lose that chance, and have to start over at a new school, where nobody even knew his name. Eventually, he was able to convince his mother to let him spend the school year in Waco with family friends.

"That was the hardest thing I ever had to do," said LT's mom. "But everything that I wanted to instill in him was already there, so I wasn't worried about it."

At first, LT liked the arrangement, since it made him feel somewhat independent. But he very quickly realized just how much he missed his mother.

"At first I thought it would be great," recalled LT. "But the more time passed, the more I realized that it wasn't as cool as I thought it would be. I found myself calling my mom sometimes just to hear the sound of her voice, and every time I wished more and more that I could be with her."

After his first game as the starting tailback, during which he scored five touchdowns, the remaining teams on University's schedule also wished that he would follow his mother and get out of town. Although he had been forced to wait in line to play tailback, once he did get his chance, he ran right into the record book.

"He was a dynamic leader," Coleman said. "He was not a big, vocal-type leader, but he was one who was going to go out and do what needed to be done and wasn't going to complain about it."

Halfway through the season, Tomlinson had already racked up more than 1,000 yards rushing, and was regularly being featured in newspaper stories and on Waco-area television stations. But as the attention grew, LT's head size remained the same.

"My mom always told me to stay humble, and not to forget where I came from," explained Tomlinson. "She always let me know while I was definitely born with talent, that if I wanted to get better, I would have to keep working hard."

By the time the season ended, Tomlinson had posted astronomical numbers, as he ran for 2,554 yards and scored 39 touchdowns, the most outstanding season by a running back that anyone in Waco had ever seen. And the numbers could have even been gaudier, but the coach pulled his young star in the fourth quarter, whenever the team was routing one of its opponents.

"He was unbelievable," said coach Coleman. "He had games where he would rush for more than 300 yards and score four or five touchdowns. He was very nearly unstoppable. But he always stayed humble, never tried to draw attention to himself the way a lot of star athletes do. He didn't make any noise, didn't do any fancy dances. He just went out and did what needed to be done.

"He was always a very down-to-earth young man," added Coleman. "He didn't change one bit, and he never complained when I took him out of games when we were blowing out opponents. He was always more interested in winning than in padding his own statistics. And he never failed to recognize the folks who helped him get there. He was always talking up his offensive linemen, and making sure that they shared in the credit for his success."

With Tomlinson piling up the points, the team won with regularity, posting a 12-2 record, its best season ever, and finished only one game shy of the state title. LT, meanwhile, was named the MVP of his district, second team all-state and the 1996 Super Centex (Central Texas) Offensive Player of the Year.

Tomlinson had been hoping that his spectacular season would draw the interest of big-time football colleges, like the University of Texas, but those schools were concerned about his size and lack of experience as a running back. In order to try to change their minds, Tomlinson played in some post-season high school all-star games. Although he didn't get any of the big schools to offer him a scholarship, he did meet another all-star who had been passed over by the large Texas schools—a quarterback from Austin by the name of Drew Brees, with whom he formed a strong and lasting bond.

Eventually, Tomlinson opted to accept a scholarship from TCU, in part because it was located in Fort Worth, an easy car ride away from his mother's apartment in Dallas. Another important factor was that Pat Sullivan, the Horned Frogs' head coach, had told LT that he would have the chance to play immediately, instead of sitting out his first year as a red-shirt freshman.

"We felt like he had a brilliant future ahead of him, as far as college went, and possibly even the NFL," said Coleman. "He's made us look very smart."

3   RUNNING SECOND

When Tomlinson arrived at TCU in the summer of 1997, he found himself backing up the Horned Frogs' junior running back, Basil Mitchell, who went on to play in a limited role for two years with the Green Bay Packers. In some ways, it was similar to the situation that he had faced in high school. The coach didn't spread out a red carpet for Tomlinson; he was going to have to earn his way on to the field, and he was going to have to wait for his turn to become the starting tailback.

But at least LT knew that he would have the chance to play, even if it was for a team whose program had been down for so long it seemed as though there wasn't any hope that it would become competitive anytime soon.

"I knew the program had gone through a rough period, but I didn't want to sit out for an entire year," said Tomlinson. "And I hoped that I could help to revive it."

Tomlinson did what he could to turn things around during that first season as Mitchell's back-up by gaining 538 yards and scoring six touchdowns on 126 carries, while adding another 107 yards on 12 pass receptions. He also became a valuable member on the kick-return unit, adding 386 yards on 20 kickoff returns to his resume. But the team was too thin on talent at too many positions to profit by Tomlinson's positive contributions, and they finished the season with a 1-10 record.

In the gloom of that sorry season, Tomlinson had provided a ray of hope, for himself as well as for the future of the team, when he ran for 180 yards and a pair of scores against Tulsa.

"One of my best memories at TCU was my breakout game against Tulsa, about halfway through my freshman season," said LT. "That performance let me know that I could play and be good at the college level."

After the season ended, the TCU athletic department decided to try to upgrade their program by hiring Dennis Franchione as the head coach. Franchione had led the New Mexico Lobos to the 1997 WAC Mountain Division championship, and it was hoped that his presence would lift TCU to similar heights.

The coaching change was welcomed by Tomlinson, who had been so discouraged by the team's bleak finish that he had thought about transferring to a different school.

"I couldn't see how things were going to get any better, but my mother calmed me down," recalled LT. "And after Franchione was hired as the head coach, I felt better. Coach Fran is like me; he hates to lose. We're similar because he's a winner, and knows what it takes to win."

At spring practice, Tomlinson showed Franchione that he could be a winner, too, and beat out Mitchell for the starting tailback role. But LT's excitement turned to disappointment in the fall of 1998, when inconsistent play by the team's fullbacks convinced Franchione to switch LT to fullback and reinstate Mitchell as the team's starting tailback. Through no fault of his own, Tomlinson had gone from being the team's main running threat, to becoming its lead blocker. The change was also painful for him because the fullback he had replaced was his best friend on the team, Lance Williams.

"It was hard, because I knew how bad Lance wanted to be in there to improve himself," said LT, who has always been a first-rate teammate. "We talked about it a lot. It was a difficult time for me."

After starting two games at fullback, however, Tomlinson was switched back to tailback, where he split time with Mitchell. During the early part of that second season with the Frogs, LT began to provide a glimpse of the greatness that would follow when he gained 206 all-purpose yards and scored a pair of touchdowns, while leading TCU to an upset win over the Falcons from the Air Force Academy, who were ranked No. 23 in the country at the time. That performance earned him the Western Athletic Conference Mountain Division Player of the Week award, and he added to his credentials the following week when he ripped off the winning score in an overtime victory against Vanderbilt.

Tomlinson finished his sophomore season with 717 rushing yards and eight TDs on 144 totes, and averaged just over 103 all-purpose yards per game. This time around, his production helped the Frogs finish in positive territory, with a 7-5 record, which was good enough to earn them an invitation to a post-season bowl game, the Sun Bowl, where they beat USC.

"He's a good back, and he has some moves," said Franchione. "He's a pretty smart football player. He studies the game and he pays attention to details."

4　THE BEST I'VE EVER SEEN

After his first two seasons at TCU, LT had run for a total of 1,255 yards, and hadn't really made an impression on the college football world. But that was about to change, and change in a big way.

During the off-season he hit the exercise room with absolute dedication, determined to develop his body as much as he could, and get his legs in shape for the upcoming season.

For Tomlinson, achieving success wasn't only a question of personal fulfillment, it was also a way to honor his mother and all that she had done for him.

"I feel like I have to pay her back by being successful," said Tomlinson, who wears a tattoo of his mother's name on his left bicep. "I feel like I owe it to her."

Tomlinson began paying off his debt to his mother by creating a season-long highlight reel, starting with the opening game of the 1999 season, when he racked up 170 yards and a score against Arizona, which boasted one of the top defenses in the nation. Two games later, he struck for 269 yards and a pair of scores against Arkansas State, and two games after that outburst he went for an even three hundred yards and another pair of scores against San Jose State, including a school record-setting 89-yard romp.

By the end of the sixth game on TCU's schedule, LT had already eclipsed the 1,000 yard mark, hitting that milestone faster than anyone else in the school's history. One of the fans in Amon Carter Stadium cheering on Tomlinson was Kenneth Davis, who had reached the 1,000-yard mark in seven games for the Frogs in 1984.

"Good for him, records are made to be broken" said Davis, who had gone on to become a high school coach in Dallas. "I'm really impressed with his ability. The kid knows how to play the game."

Just how well Tomlinson knew the game became apparent in TCU's next-to-last game of the regular season, when he ran absolutely wild against the University of Texas-El Paso's hapless defense. In a display of running brilliance that might be the most astonishing performance ever by a tailback in a college football game, LT ripped through and dodged around the UTEP defenders for 406 rushing yards, which still stands as the most rushing yards ever recorded in a single game by a Division 1 player.

"He just out-ran us, made cuts and, boom, he was gone," said UTEP coach Charlie Bailey, who had stood helpless on the sideline during LT's record-setting performance. "Basically, they just lined up, gave him the ball, and he stuck it down our throats. We didn't have any answers for Tomlinson."

LT had already rushed for 119 yards by halftime, but the Frogs went into the locker room tied at 17-17. The coaching staff knew that they needed a win to preserve their conference title hopes and bowl game dreams, and they decided that the best way to achieve those goals was to ride LT as often as he could stand to carry the ball in the second half.

"An assistant coach came over to me at halftime and

said, "Get ready to roll, because we're going to keep calling your number," recalled Tomlinson, who wound up toting the ball a TCU record 43 times. "But I didn't realize just how many carries he was talking about."

LT found out just how literal the coach had been when he heard his number called on all but one of TCU's first 17 plays in the third quarter, a strategy that produced a pair of TDs and sparked the team to a 54-24 romp.

"Going into the game, I really wasn't thinking about running for a lot of yards," said Tomlinson, who not only broke the record of 396 rushing yards that had been set in 1991, but also scored six touchdowns, including long-distance sprints of 63 and 70 yards. "A really good day would be 300 yards and three touchdowns. Six touchdowns are amazing. I really never dreamed of doing that. I saw Ricky Williams do it a couple of times when he played for Texas, but I really never thought about doing it."

Coach Franchione, who had been as surprised as everyone else by what he had just seen, was left almost speechless.

"That's the best performance by a running back that I've ever seen," said the coach. "I don't know what else there is to say. I've watched a lot of college football and I haven't seen any back do what he did."

The only disappointing part about the day for LT was the fact that his mother hadn't been in the stands—as she usually was for TCU's home games—because she was watching LaVar play in a high school playoff game.

"I looked up in the stands and wished my mom was there, but at least she knew what was going on," said

Tomlinson. "She was listening to the game on the radio and jumping around in the stands at my brother's game. People there thought she was crazy."

Although LT's mom wasn't there to watch him, TCU quarterback Patrick Batteaux could hardly take his eyes off his teammate.

"He certainly made my job a whole lot easier," said Batteaux, whose role was, mainly, reduced to handing off the ball to LT and then faking another move. "I still had to carry out my fakes, but it was kind of hard because I wanted to watch him run, just like everybody else."

Thanks in large part to LT's incredible playmaking, the Frogs closed the season at 8-4—the school's best record in four decades—which included a 28-14 win over East Carolina in the Mobile Alabama Bowl.

Tomlinson's highlight reel of a season allowed him to lead the nation in rushing with 1,850 yards—16 ahead of Wisconsin's Ron Dayne—and break the TCU single-season record of 1,611, which had been set by Kenneth Davis in 1984.

His season-long display of brilliance was so dominating that he was named the WAC Offensive Player of the Week five times in 11 games by the conference's coaches, and he was the unanimous choice as the WAC Offensive Player of the Year. His exploits also earned him recognition on the national stage, where he finished fourth in voting for the 1999 Doak Walker Award, which is given annually to the best running back in Division 1.

The only down note in a season filled with high ones occurred the week before Tomlinson's record-setting performance against UTEP, when the Frogs beat North Texas 27-3. LT had been excited but nervous before the start of the game, because he knew that for the first time since he had played in a Pee Wee League contest, his father was in the stands.

Unfortunately, that was one game in which LT didn't shine brightly, so instead of celebrating the victory with his teammates, LT sat slumped in front of his locker, weeping because he had rushed for only 75 yards.

5   GAINING YARDS AND GIVING BACK

After Tomlinson's spectacular junior season he started to receive a great deal of media attention, and he was also selected for a large number of pre-season All-American squads, including one that involved a photo shoot with the other players that had been chosen for the team. LT welcomed the opportunity to reconnect with Drew Brees, who had gone on to become a star at Purdue, and to meet the other gifted athletes, especially Michael Vick, the Virginia Tech quarterback, who many people considered to be the favorite to win the 2000 Heisman Trophy, the most famous and coveted of the post-season college player-of-the-year awards.

As soon as he and Vick met, the quarterback showed that he had been thinking about the meeting as well.

"First thing he said to me was, 'How did you rush for 400 yards in one game,'" said Tomlinson. "You know, I guess that's when I first really understood the magnitude of the accomplishment."

Tomlinson appreciated the fact that his record-setting performance had raised his profile and placed him on the radar screen of NFL teams, but he also started to feel as if his singular achievement had become something of an albatross.

"I'm a little tired of just being known as the guy who ran for 400 yards," said LT. "There's more to my game than that. I want people to know that I can catch the ball and block, too."

Tomlinson, however, didn't have to be concerned that his all-around talents were being obscured by that one game. In fact, he, in addition to Vick and along with Brees and a few others, was considered one of the leading contenders for the Heisman.

The athletic department at TCU jumped on the Heisman bandwagon with both feet—seeing the publicity not only as a chance to boost Tomlinson's candidacy, but also as a vehicle to entice future high school stars to want to play for the Horned Frogs. The school's publicity machine filled the city of Fort Worth with a sea of posters and billboards with LT's face on them, and circulated tens of thousands of purple bumper stickers proclaiming, *LT for Heisman.*

With all the talk about his Heisman credentials, LT couldn't help but do a bit of daydreaming, although he realized that TCU would have to post a winning record for him to have a legitimate shot at winning the trophy.

"It's nice that people are thinking so highly of me, but I know that I have a lot of hard work ahead of me," said LT. "I also know that the team will have to do well, regardless of how well I do as an individual, because not too many people are going to vote for a player who plays for a mediocre team."

Although Tomlinson was happy to be considered among college football's elite performers, and welcomed the challenge of competing for its most famous award, he didn't relish all the attention that came with being a celebrity.

"When you're growing up, you look at top athletes as

being like gods," said Tomlinson. "When you get to that point and people start looking at you that way, it's an unbelievable feeling. But it's also strange, and I haven't gotten used to it."

As a result of all the hoopla, Tomlinson spent more time than he would have liked giving interviews to radio and television broadcasters, and a seemingly endless line of newspaper and magazine reporters. But, as always, he treated each person with the same respect with which he would have wanted to be treated if the situations were reversed.

"One of my prayers was that he would stay humble through this process, and he has," said his mom. "The person you see today is the same person that LaDainian was as a child."

Tomlinson also put his celebrity to good use, employing it to reach out to children in the Fort Worth community by volunteering with the local Boys and Girls Clubs, as well as visiting schools and talking to students through TCU's School to Goal program.

"I remember when I was growing up and older guys would come in and talk," explained LT, who also starred in a motivational video, *Score a Goal in the Classroom*, and was featured on billboards on behalf of *Teachers are the Real Heroes* campaign. "I looked up to them and learned so much. For me, it didn't have to be a football player or somebody who was famous; just somebody who was older and had gone through what I was going through and understood what it was about. That taught me how important it was to have role models. So now, I get a kick being on the other side of that situation, hoping that I'm making a difference to some kids.

"Sometimes a kid will come up to me and say, 'I'm not good enough' or 'my coach says I'm not good enough.' I try to make them understand that that just means you have to work harder, because you can't ever let somebody else stop you from doing what you love.

"My basic message to them is to have fun and work hard," added LT. "I was always encouraged to just do my best, and that's the lesson that I try to pass on."

While the sports world is filled with people who allow attention to swell their heads and then start to think that they're more important than their teammates, coach Franchione knew that LT would stay grounded and not be knocked off balance by his status.

"If LT was a different type of person, all the attention he's receiving might be a problem," said the coach. "But I have never seen one bit of selfishness from that young man. He's unselfish and he cares a great deal for his teammates."

Tomlinson validated that opinion at a team meeting held in August, when Franchione presented him with the plaque he had earned for being the leading rusher in Division 1-A the previous year. As soon as Franchione handed him the award, LT turned it over to his offensive linemen—a group that he affectionately referred to as 'The Big Uglies'—as his way of honoring them for their part in having helped him win the rushing title.

"That's really all you need to know about LT," said David Bobo, who was an offensive tackle. "He's not only our best player, he's also one of the best people."

6   THE LAST TIME AROUND

As LT waited for his final season at TCU to begin, he couldn't help but take some peeks at how Michael Vick and Drew Brees had started their seasons.

"Watching them on television will make me play harder," said Tomlinson, as though he needed any extra incentive to squeeze out every last ounce of talent and effort from himself. "It's going to be a lot of fun."

The fun, actually, started for TCU before the season's opening game, when they were ranked among the nation's top 25 teams for the first time in more than 10 years.

"We're excited about our ranking," said Franchione. "It's a sign of respect for our accomplishments over the past two seasons. However, it's not where you start, but where you finish that determines whether you've had a successful season."

TCU added to its rising tide of respect by starting the season with a 41-10 rout of Nevada, as Tomlinson rushed for 176 yards and three touchdowns before leaving the game in the third quarter.

While 100-yards rushing in a game is generally considered to be the standard of excellence for a running back, Tomlinson turned the century mark into a commonplace by rushing for at least 100 yards in every game during the 2000 season. He also scored at least one touchdown in each game, while scoring two or more in seven of them.

The Frogs continued their roll by trouncing North-western 41-14, as Tomlinson exploded for 243 yards and a pair of scores.

"I could have had 350," said LT, who had lost out on another pair of TDs and 108 yards because of two holding penalties. "But I feel as though I still played well."

It was amazing that Tomlinson could feel anything at all after he'd carried the ball 39 times, but he did so without complaint.

"I like having the ball in my hands," said LT. "I like trying to make things happen, whether it's hitting the home run on one play, or it's going down the field, one carry at a time."

Tomlinson wasn't the only one who was pleased that the ball was so often in his hands. For coach Franchione, LT's hands were as comforting as a security blanket.

"Ideally, we would like to have a balanced offense," said Franchione. "But when you have a guy like LaDainian, you want to get him the ball as often as possible."

Sometimes, though, when the Horned Frogs were way ahead of their opponents, LT took himself out of the game and allowed his backups to get some playing time, even though he knew that sitting on the sidelines could reduce his chances of winning the Heisman.

"It kind of reminds me of my senior year in high school, when I didn't play in the fourth quarter of half the games," said LT. "Obviously, the Heisman goes by numbers, and the voters won't really know that I didn't play the fourth quarter. But that's fine with me, as long as we keep winning."

Although some NFL scouts had questioned Tomlinson's ability to run between the tackles, Jerry Brown,

Northwestern's defensive coordinator didn't notice any deficiencies in LT's ability to run through the big trees on the defensive line.

"That's the big difference between Tomlinson last year and this year," said Brown. "This year he ran inside on us with power and evasiveness. He wasn't just adequate, he was outstanding."

The Frogs demolished their third successive opponent by stampeding Arkansas State 52-3, giving the team its eighth consecutive win going back to 1999, the school's longest winning streak since 1938, the year it had won its last national title. Tomlinson did his part to keep the party going by rushing for 140 yards and another pair of scores.

TCU then whitewashed a stubborn Navy team, 24-0, as LT picked up another score and 121 yards rushing, to become the school's career rushing leader, with 3,785 yards. The Frogs continued on their roll the following week by hammering Hawaii 41-21, as LT rambled for 294 yards and four touchdowns. It was another record-breaking day for Tomlinson, who set new school marks for career points (264), career all-purpose yards (5,136), and single-game rushing attempts (49).

"I checked the chart at halftime and saw that he had 31 carries in the first half, and I thought, 'Boy, I'm really running my horse,'" said Franchione with a smile, as his team improved to 5-0 and continued its climb in the national polls. "I didn't want to tire him out, but I knew he could handle the load. In fact, I think that he gets better with more touches. He likes the ball, and I like seeing him run with it."

The win for the 5-0 Horned Frogs was their 10th

straight over two seasons, the longest winning streak for the school since a 14-game winning streak in 1937-38. It was the first time they had started a season at 5-0 since 1942.

TCU continued on its winning ways, and LT continued to pile up huge chunks of yardage, as the Frogs toppled Tulsa and Rice, which raised their winning streak to 12 games, the longest in the nation.

"It's amazing to just think about having a 7-0 record and being ranked ninth in the country," said LT, who had scored twice and toted the ball for 200 yards against Rice. "From where we were four years ago, it's really unbelievable. Back then, when we were 1-10, I remember thinking about the teams that were undefeated, and trying to imagine what that would be like. I guarantee you there's no way anybody here could have guessed that we would be in that position three years later."

What made the game especially rewarding for LT was that his father, who was 65 years old at the time, had come to see him play, and that this time Tomlinson didn't end the game in tears.

"This was more like it," said LT afterwards, a big smile stretched across his face.

The smile faded a bit the following week, however, as the Frogs' dreams of an undefeated season were stopped by San Jose State, 27-24. TCU bounced right back in its next game against Fresno State, however, as LT notched a 65-yard TD run. The Frogs then went on to demolish UTEP, 47-14, as LT racked up a season-high 305 rushing yards and a trio of TDs in the final home game of his college career.

His 68-yard scoring jaunt in the first quarter made

him the WAC's all-time leading rusher, and his 89-yard scoring dash in the third quarter, equaled his career high. The three scores gave him 21 for the season, breaking the record of 18 that had been set by Jim Swink in 1955 and matched by LT in 1999.

"I knew nobody was going to catch me today," said LT afterwards. "Towards the end of the game I was thinking that I couldn't have dreamed of a better way to end my career at Amon Carter Stadium."

"He's probably the best running back in the country," said UTEP coach Gary Nord. "He breaks tackles, has great balance and speed, and he sees the field as well as any back I've ever coached against."

There was only one game left in the regular season, a meeting against SMU, in Dallas, and a win would give the Frogs their second consecutive conference championship. Tomlinson, meanwhile, was only 16 yards away from reaching 2,000 rushing yards for the season, but the most significant aspect about the game for LT was that it was going to be the first time that his entire family—his mother, father, sister and brother—were going to be in the stands watching him play.

"I've waited a long time for this day," said LT. "Having them all at the game means more to me than I can say."

The game quickly turned into a blowout, as the Frogs swamped SMU 62-7, while LT put on a dazzling show for his family with a 74-yard touchdown run, and finished the day with 2,158 rushing yards, the fourth-highest single-season total in NCAA history. Tomlinson, who had also wrapped up his second straight rushing title, joined Ricky Williams as the only two running backs to register 2,000 rushing yards in a season and 5,000 for a career.

After his last carry of the day, TCU called timeout, and Tomlinson walked slowly toward the sideline, as though he was reluctant to bring his storied regular season career to an end. As the crowd rose and cheered, coach Franchione wrapped his arms around his star running back, and then, one by one, the entire team embraced LT.

"Those were very emotional moments for me," said LT, who ended his career with 5,263 rushing yards, the most ever in the WAC conference, and the sixth-best in NCAA history. "I thought about the long road I had traveled from my Pee Wee league days, and about how far the seniors on this team had come from our freshman year, when we were 1-10, to achieve a 10-1 record. It was an overwhelming feeling."

Not even a wrenching loss in the Mobile Alabama Bowl to Southern Mississippi, who scored the winning points with only eight seconds left in the game, could dim the brilliance of LT's All-American senior season. Although Tomlinson didn't win the Heisman Trophy—he finished fourth, behind three quarterbacks, including Drew Brees, who finished third, but two spots ahead of Michael Vick—he was named the WAC Player of the Year for the second straight season. He also won the 2000 Doak Walker Award, which is given annually to the best running back in the country, based upon voting by national media members and former running backs.

"LaDainian did incredible things on the field during the season, but his work with teachers and students was just as impressive," said Skeeter Walker, the widow of Doak Walker, a former SMU and NFL running back and the winner of the 1948 Heisman Trophy. "He exemplifies Doak's spirit of sportsmanship and citizenship, and is an excellent representative for the Award and for college football."

7 RECORD-SETTING ROOKIE

In spite of his two rushing titles and stack of record-setting performances, a number of NFL scouts still had questions about Tomlinson's ability to be a playmaker at the next level. To answer those questions, Tomlinson turned in an MVP Award-winning performance at the Senior Bowl, a post-season all-star game, and followed that up with impressive workouts at the NFL combine, where prospects get their last chance to impress the league's talent evaluators before the draft of college players.

As the big day approached, LT traveled to New York, where the draft usually takes place, living out a fantasy he had imagined since he was a young boy.

"I dreamed about being in the green room, waiting for my name to be called out, wearing a suit and then putting on a team's hat," recalled LT. "That it's actually going to be happening is overwhelming for me."

The San Diego Chargers had owned the No. 1 pick in the 2001 draft because they had finished the 2000 season with an NFL-worst 1-15 record. Most experts had guessed that they'd use the pick to take Michael Vick, but the Chargers' general manager at the time, John Butler, wound up trading the choice to Atlanta for the Falcons' first round pick, No. 5 overall, two other draft choices, and the rights to Tim Dwight, a speedy wide receiver and punt returner.

The Bolts used that No. 5 slot to take LT, and then

addressed their future quarterback needs by selecting Drew Brees in the second round. Although he knew that the Chargers were a terrible team, Tomlinson approached this new challenge with his usual enthusiasm and determination.

"At TCU we were 1-10 in my freshman year, so I know what it takes to go in and help rebuild a program," noted LT. "It takes hard work and dedication, and I'm on board with that. I've set my goals high and I look forward to doing positive things for the team."

The Bolts didn't waste any time in testing LT's resolve, as quarterback Doug Flutie handed off the ball to him 36 times in the Bolts' 30-3 opening game win against Washington. LT responded to the heavy workload by piling up 113 yards and a pair of touchdowns before a cheering crowd in San Diego's Qualcomm Stadium.

"He showed some toughness," said Junior Seau, the team's All-Pro middle linebacker. "He did a heck of a job, running for over 100 yards in his first game. That's hard to do in this league, especially against a defense as tough as theirs."

The happiest fan in Qualcomm that day had to be LT's mom, who had also made the trip to Arizona to see her son play in the team's final exhibition game.

"I told her, 'Mom, it's only a pre-season game, and I'm not going to get many carries,'" recalled LT. "But she said, 'I don't care. I remember when you were a kid and you used to tell me you were going to make it to the NFL. I don't care if it is a pre-season game. You're still my baby, and I'm going to be there when you step on the field for the first time."

Similar thoughts streamed through Tomlinson's mind when he ran on to the field at Qualcomm for his first regular season game.

"As soon as I ran on to the field, it hit me, and I had a tear in my eye," said Tomlinson. "This is something I've dreamed about since I was a little kid, and I got emotional. I just thought to myself, "I've made it. Then, I wiped the tears and said to myself, 'Let's do it.'"

The emotional roller coaster continued into the next game for LT, which was at Texas Stadium, a place where he had sometimes sat, high up in the rafters, to watch and cheer for Emmitt Smith and the Cowboys.

"Oh my goodness, it was unbelievable as a kid to sit in the stands," recalled LT, before the game. "I grew up watching Emmitt. I went to his football camp. It's going to be unbelievably exciting to be on the same field with him."

The two players had, in fact, become friendly over the years, and the admiration flowed in both directions.

"LaDainian is a great kid," said Smith, who had called to congratulate LT after his game against Washington. "And he has a chance to become a great back in this league."

Although the Bolts won the game, Smith had a special moment near the end of the first half, when he ran for 14 yards and passed the retired Barry Sanders for second place on the all-time career-rushing list with 15,291 yards. Only Walter Payton, who had rushed for 16,726 yards in his Hall of Fame career, stood between Smith and the record.

The Chargers were back home the following week,

and LT lit the fuse by racking up 107 yards and a trio of scores, as the Bolts beat the Cincinnati Bengals, 28-14.

"I expected to come in and do well," said Tomlinson, who had scored an NFL-high six touchdowns, and been named the AFC Rookie of the Month for September. "I'm not a cocky person, but I believe I've been blessed with an ability to play football. I work hard, use my talent, and let the results speak for themselves."

The play of LT on offense and a stingy defensive unit seemed to fill the team with confidence, and allowed the holdovers from 2000 to believe that they could put that nightmarish season behind them.

"We just want to let the league know that this is a new year and we're a different team," said linebacker Orlando Ruff. "We've moved forward and the teams on our schedule better be ready for us."

Their winning streak came to an end the following week, however, when the Bolts were beaten by the Cleveland Browns, 20-16, despite another standout performance by LT. But the Chargers rallied to take two of their next three games and, at 5-2, they looked as though they might be ready to make a run at a division title or, at least, play their way into the post-season.

But their smooth sailing sloop became swamped by a tidal wave of nine straight losses, which left them shipwrecked with a 5-11 record, and a familiar spot at the bottom of the AFC West standings.

As the Bolts' season was being sunk by their poor play, the yards became harder for LT to gain. After he'd rushed for over 100 yards in three of the team's first four games, he didn't hit the century mark again for 10 straight games. Despite the falloff, he continued to make a solid contribution and confirm his position as one of the league's top rookies.

His 13 catches against Arizona in the 11th game of the season, for example, were the most ever by a Bolts' back, and the third-most in franchise history. In an early December game against the Seattle Seahawks he scored his tenth TD, which set a Chargers' rookie record, and the following week he went over the 1,000-yard mark against the Eagles in Philadelphia. But all the losing made his personal accomplishments taste somewhat bitter-sweet.

"It's tough to think about getting 1,000 yards when you lose the game," said Tomlinson, after he'd become the first Charger rookie since 1974 to rush for more than 1,000 yards. "It's hard to swallow all those losses."

In the next-to-last week of the regular season, LT bounced back, even if the team didn't, and he ripped the Kansas City Chiefs for a season-high 145 rushing yards, which brought his total to a franchise rookie record 1,198 yards rushing, and broke the record of 1,162 that had been set by Don Woods in 1974.

"It felt good to get 100 yards again," said LT. "But don't give me all the credit, I had a lot of help out there."

Of course, there isn't a back in the world who can run for significant yardage without competent blocking, but his coaches and teammates knew that LT did a bit more than just follow his blockers.

"He's come into this league at a very high level," said Ollie Wilson, the running backs coach. "Rookies don't do what he's doing right now."

Tomlinson, who was named the Bolts' Offensive Player of the Year and the Associated Press Offensive Rookie of the Year, went on to finish his first season in the NFL ranked fifth in the AFC in rushing and fourth in combined yards from scrimmage. He led all the league's rookies in rushing yardage, with 1,236, the most ever by a Bolts' rookie; rushing touchdowns (10), rushing attempts (339) and combined yards from scrimmage, with 1,603, breaking the 36-year-old franchise record of 1,590 that had been set by Hall of Fame receiver Lance Alworth, who had totaled his yardage in only a 14-game schedule.

"The record is fine, it's good for my confidence," said Tomlinson. "It means a lot to me and the guys who helped me get it. But I just wish I could have gotten it in a winning season, when it would mean more."

Tomlinson's attitude and team-first approach counted as much with his teammates as his running ability.

"He's a great running back, but I'm just as proud of the maturity he's shown this season," said Rodney Harrison, who was the Chargers' Pro Bowl strong safety. "He's going to shatter many records before his career is over."

8   DREAMS AND NIGHTMARES

The Chargers' dismal finish convinced John Butler to fire Mike Riley, whose Chargers' teams had posted a 14-34 record in his three seasons as head coach. In his place, they brought in the highly respected Marty Schottenheimer, who had experienced only one losing season in his 16 years as an NFL head coach.

Tomlinson, meanwhile, arrived at training camp determined to improve on his outstanding rookie season and help turn the Bolts into a winning team.

"My primary goal is to help get the team into the playoffs," said Tomlinson. "That's my top priority. On a personal level, my goal is to lead the league in rushing, and I'm looking forward to accomplishing that goal. I learned a lot last year about what the defenses are trying to do, and I want to use that knowledge to take my game to another level."

The team opened the 2002 season with Drew Brees as the starting quarterback and with three straight wins, but they hadn't beaten a quality team, so no one really knew if they were for real, or if they had just been feeding on the weak. Most commentators, such as ESPN football analyst Sean Salisbury, who called the Chargers "pretenders, not contenders," thought that the Bolts' bubble would burst in week four, when they took on the defending Super Bowl champion New England Patriots, who rode a 12-game winning streak into Qualcomm Stadium.

The Chargers turned out to be rude hosts, however, as they posted a 21-14 win over the Pats, with LT supplying 217 rushing yards and two long touchdown runs.

"No one gave us a chance to win," said an exultant Tomlinson afterwards. "When I came out on the field today, I was steamed by all the negative talk about us, and I just wanted to prove a point."

"When you've got LaDainian Tomlinson, it's hard not to keep calling running plays," said Schottenheimer, who had called only 18 passing plays. "Every time he gets the ball, he has a chance to take it into the end zone."

After a loss to the Denver Broncos, the Bolts bounced back with wins over the Chiefs and the Raiders, as LT racked up a 19-yard game-winning TD run against Oakland.

"They should put that run on ESPN Classics right now," said fullback Fred McCrary, whose block had helped to spring Tomlinson's dash to the end zone. "It will definitely stand the test of time."

While Tomlinson knew that the weight of the offense was on his shoulders, he carried the responsibility like a badge of honor, rather than as a burden.

"I've been doing it all my life," said LT. "I'm actually comfortable with the role, more so than I would be if I was just a role player. I'm ready for the challenge."

Although the Bolts were running hard and leading the AFC West division, general manager John Butler waved a cautionary flag.

"I'm pleased with where we are, but there's still a long ways to go," noted Butler. "This team is loaded with first- and second-year players, who aren't used to a 16-game schedule yet. Once we get to the 12th game and beyond, the grind may sap them both mentally and physically."

The Chargers had counted on winning their next game, since they would be at home and playing the New York Jets, who came into the contest with a 2-5 record and the lowest-ranked run-defense in the NFL. But the Jets blew out the Bolts 44-13, a loss that angered and embarrassed the team.

"We played poorly and got what we deserved," said Schottenheimer. "As hard as it is to swallow, that's the reality of it. But we're going to bounce back and play well. I have no doubt about that."

Tomlinson tried to soften the loss by reminding people of how far the team had come in half a season.

"If someone would have said that we'd be 6-2 at the halfway point of the season, we would have been happy with that," said LT. "I'm sure that there are a lot of people in San Diego and around the country who are surprised at where we're at. But we know we have a good team, and we expect to finish strong."

But the Bolts started the second half of the season with a painful loss at St. Louis, when the Rams torched the Bolts' secondary for a pair of touchdown passes in the final 3:06 of the game. Suddenly, it seemed as if some of the players had started looking over their shoulders at the 2001 collapse, and they began speaking as if they could hear the footsteps of another debacle coming toward them.

"We don't want anyone, player or fan, to think this is anything like last year," said defensive end Marcus Wiley, who sounded as though he was trying to keep his own fears at bay by talking about them. "So we've got to change those thoughts by going out and winning a game."

Which is exactly what the Bolts did, as they stifled the San Francisco 49ers in overtime, 20-17, when Steve Christie sliced the uprights with a 40-yard field goal.

"It shows what kind of heart this team has, to keep battling and win a game like this," said LT, who went over the 1,000-yard rushing mark. "There are no quitters in this locker room."

But the team's offensive unit, which had been soft for a month, completely melted away the following week in Miami, as the Bolts were dominated by the Dolphins' defense in a 30-3 loss. The offense had, in fact, scored only five touchdowns in the previous four games, and the Bolts, unsurprisingly, had lost three of them.

As a result, their immediate future looked bleak, because the Bolts' next game was against the Broncos, who had the highest-rated run defense in the NFL. But Chargers' fullback Fred McCrary, LT's lead blocker, seemed undaunted by the challenge of winning the battle on the ground.

"I think we can run the ball on them," said McCrary. "I know they're No.1 against the run, but running the ball is our strength. So, let's get ready to roll."

No one was more ready than LT, who rocked Denver's defense for a team-record 220 yards and a couple of touchdowns on the ground, and added another 51 yards and a third score on 11 pass receptions, as the Bolts beat the Broncos 30-27, in OT.

"He's a great running back, right up there with Emmitt," said Bolts' guard Kelvin Garmon, a former teammate of Smith's in Dallas. "Even when we messed up and missed our blocks, he just bounced off of tacklers and kept going."

The three touchdowns upped LT's season total to 13, making him only the 11th player in league history to score 10 or more in each of his first two seasons. With 1,318 rushing yards, LT had already eclipsed his rookie total and was only four yards behind Kansas City's Priest Holmes for the league lead.

With the win, the Bolts broke the tie for the division lead they had shared with the Broncos, and stood atop the AFC West with an 8-4 record.

But as it turned out, that was the high water mark for the Chargers, who stumbled to the end of the season with four straight losses, which left them with an 8-8 record and out of the playoff picture. The collapse was even more painful than the one they had endured the previous year, because everyone realized that the 2001 team didn't have enough talent to become a serious contender. But this time around, there wasn't a player or coach who hadn't thought that the Bolts would play in the post-season and end the franchise's six-year playoff drought.

"I can't even believe the season is over," said LT, after the last whistle of 2002 had been blown. "I feel like we should still be playing; the season shouldn't be over."

Although the Chargers had suffered their second successive season of meltdown, Tomlinson continued his run toward greatness, as he rushed for a franchise-record 1,683 yards, second in the NFL behind Ricky Williams, and added 489 yards on 79 receptions, which tied the Charger's mark for receptions by a running back. For his accomplishments, Tomlinson, who also scored 15 touchdowns, was named to the AFC Pro Bowl squad, fulfilling one of his boyhood fantasies.

"When I got the news, at first I couldn't believe it," said LT. "It's something I've always dreamed about."

But his personal accomplishments didn't compensate for the pain he felt at the team's inability to play winning football on a consistent basis.

"I don't play this game for myself, I play to win championships, and I'm sick and tired of losing," said LT, dispirited by the nightmare of another dismal ending. "I don't know how much longer I can take this."

9 GREATNESS AMONG THE RUINS

The off-season turned out to be one of the most wrenching in team history, starting with the death of general manager John Butler, who was replaced by his longtime assistant, A.J. Smith.

The Chargers tried to address their defensive deficiencies in a peculiar way when they parted with their two most-decorated defensive players, linebacker Junior Seau, who was traded to Miami, and safety Rodney Harrison, whom they chose not to re-sign.

"If they feel like they'll be better without me, that's their decision, but I'm going to go somewhere else and make whomever I sign with a better team," said Harrison, who went on to anchor the New England Patriots' secondary.

The Chargers moved to improve their offense, which had ranked only 16th in the league in 2002, despite LT's astonishing accomplishments, by signing a pair of relatively high-profile free agents: wide receiver David Boston and fullback Lorenzo Neal, widely considered to be the best blocking back in the NFL. The Bolts also signed a college basketball player, Antonio Gates, with the intention of turning him into a tight end, a move that would pay big dividends down the road.

After he'd taken some time to recover from the team's complete collapse in 2002, Tomlinson had begun to prepare for the 2003 season with a grueling workout regimen.

"There's not a player in the NFL who works as hard as I do," said Tomlinson. "If I didn't commit to making a total effort, I would be cheating myself and the team. If I'm going to play the game, I want to leave a mark on it, become the best running back ever, and help the Chargers win Super Bowls.

"This year, I think everything is in place for this team to be really good," he continued. "If we could just make it to the playoffs, then we'd gain the confidence to start a winning tradition here."

But the Bolts quickly showed that they weren't even close to being good by opening the season with five straight losses.

"I don't have any answers, just frustration," said LT, after he'd run for 187 yards and one score, and also thrown a touchdown pass, in a loss at Oakland. "It's wasted. I can't enjoy it; we're still losers."

The Bolts finally won their first game in their sixth try, when they beat the Browns, 26-20, as LT ran for a score and 200 yards, including a 57-yard romp that left defenders grasping at air.

"When I cut back, I saw the cornerback coming at me, so I knew I could take it outside," said LT, who had run for 200 yards or more three times in his first 38 games in the league, breaking the record of Hall of Famer Earl Campbell, who had taken 41 games to do it. "When I cut back up the field, it was just all about breaking tackles, and after that it was off to the races.

"You want your teammates to depend on you, and when they do, you need to come up with the plays," said LT. "You need to back up your talk with results."

Some of those teammates, though, took exception to

Tomlinson's decision to wear a Junior Seau Miami Dolphins' jersey to practice the week before the Fish handed the Chargers their sixth loss in seven games.

"Everyone's entitled to their own opinion, including me," said Tomlinson, who stood behind his decision to honor a player who had earned 12 Pro Bowl selections in his 13 seasons in San Diego. "I wanted to honor Junior for what he did for me and what he did for the game. You have to respect people who have done as much as he has. It's no different than if I wore a Bo Jackson or Joe Montana jersey. It's all about being respectful."

In the fourth quarter of the Charger's next game, a 20-7 loss at Chicago, Schottenheimer decided to pull the reins away from Brees and put the team back in the hands of Doug Flutie. The move seemed to pay off the following week, when Flutie passed for a pair of touchdowns and scrambled for two more, as the Bolts beat the Minnesota Vikings, 42-27.

"It makes it a lot easier to run when the defense has to pay attention to other people," said Tomlinson, who had racked up 162 yards and two touchdowns, including a career-best 73-yarder. "It was really balanced, and that's how you play winning football."

But the joy and balance vanished the following week, as the Broncos bottled up the Bolts, 37-8. It seemed as though all the wheels came off the bus in this game, as Flutie played like the 41-year-old he was, and the Chargers' coaching staff held LT in check by limiting him to only eight carries, a career-low.

"There's a difference between talking about pride and showing it on the field," said Tomlinson, who was furious at the lackadaisical play of some of his teammates, and frustrated at his lack of touches.

"Since I've been playing football, we've never dominated a team like we did today, not at the NFL level," said Denver linebacker Al Wilson, acknowledging that the fight had gone out of the 2-8 Bolts.

After losses to Cincinnati and Kansas City, the Bolts beat the Detroit Lions, 14-7, as Tomlinson ran for 88 yards and caught nine passes for 148 yards—a season-high for running backs—and the team's only two scores.

"We just want to finish on a positive note," said LT, his lofty dreams of making the playoffs replaced by a desire to at least salvage some scraps from a lost season. "We won one game and we're going to try to put a streak together."

But the Bolts, with Brees back at quarterback, lost their next two games before they closed out their 4-12 season with a 21-14 win over the Raiders. Although the game was meaningless, LT played as though a title was at stake, as he carried the ball 31 times and gained a franchise-record 243 rushing yards.

Despite the dismal performance of many of the players surrounding him, Tomlinson added another spectacular season to his résumé by becoming the first back in NFL history to rush for 1,000 yards and catch 100 passes in a single season. His final numbers included 1,645 rushing yards, good for 13 touchdowns, and 725 receiving yards and four scores. The 2,370 total yards were the second-most in NFL history, behind only Marshall Faulk, who had totaled 2,429 yards for the Rams in 1999.

"The guy is absolutely the most remarkable athlete I've ever been around," said Schottenheimer. "The young man goes out there and performs every day, in practice as well as in games. I have been doing this a long time—back to 1965 as a player—and I have never seen anyone like him."

10   BREAKTHROUGH

Shortly before the start of the 2004 season, a poll of NFL executives ranked Tomlinson as the No. 1 player in the league, a result that hadn't surprised Chargers' owner Alex Spanos.

"He's not just the best running back in the NFL," said Spanos, who had recently signed LT to a six-year contract that made him the highest-paid running back in league history. "He's a superstar on and off the field, and the heart and soul of our organization."

Although LT's greatness was a given, most of the preseason publications had still picked the Bolts to finish at or near the bottom of their division. Tomlinson, though, shrugged off those predictions as though they were opposing cornerbacks.

"We'll just use that for motivation," said LT, as the team prepared to fly to Houston for its opening game against the Texans. "Every year there are teams that move to the forefront of their division. We've put in the hard work and dedication, so why not us? You have to believe. If you don't believe, you've already lost."

The Bolts got off on the right foot by beating the Texans, but they lost their next two games, in large part because of the ineffectiveness of Drew Brees.

"It just gets harder and harder to swallow," said Tomlinson, who could feel the season slipping away. "At the same time, you have to go into every game thinking you have a shot at it. You never know when you're going to break out and start a streak."

The Bolts did win their next game, beating the Tennessee Titans, as Brees finally got up to speed and Tomlinson piled up 147 yards on the ground.

"Drew was very decisive today," said LT, who became the franchise's career rushing leader with 4,979 yards, breaking the record that had been set by Paul Lowe, who played for the Chargers from 1960-68. "When the whole offense is clicking the way it was today, it makes everybody's job easier."

The Bolts won again the following week when they toppled the Jacksonville Jaguars 34-21, although LT limped off the field late in the third quarter with a groin injury that would limit his production for the next four games. But they followed that win with a painful loss in Atlanta, as Michael Vick rallied the Falcons with two fourth-quarter touchdowns that earned them a 21-20 win.

Instead of allowing the defeat to crush them, the Chargers closed out the first half of the season with two straight wins, which upped their record to 5-3. Then, they opened the second half of their schedule with a 43-17 thumping of the New Orleans Saints, with Brees clicking on four scoring passes, including three to Antonio Gates, who had become one of the top pass-catching tight ends in the NFL.

"We have more experience on offense, and it's wide open now," said LT. "Defenses can't just load up against the run; they have to worry about us throwing the ball."

With extra time off due to the bye-week, LT's groin injury finally healed, and he helped power the Bolts to another win over Oakland, 23-17. As a result of his return to full strength, LT regained the explosiveness and cutting ability that had been missing in the previous four games, and he was able to rock the Raiders for 164 yards, a season high.

"Last years, we lost these types of games," said LT, whose fourth quarter TD run had provided the Chargers with their margin of victory. "This team has come a long way."

The Bolts continued on their roll by beating Kansas City, 34-31 and then Denver, 20-17, as LT galloped for 113 yards and the team's only two TDs of the day. The win assured the Chargers of finishing the season with a winning record, but they weren't satisfied with that meager accomplishment.

"Our goal wasn't to simply have a winning season," said safety Jerry Wilson. "Our goal was to go a long, long way. But we know if we keep winning that we'll take the division title."

The Bolts upped their winning streak to seven games by beating the Tampa Bay Buccaneers, 31-24, as linebacker Donnie Edwards picked off a pass and took it to the house for the winning points.

"Our defense won this game for us," said Tomlinson. "There are times when we need our defense to carry us, and there are times when the defense will lean on us. That's what being a team is all about."

The following week, on a cold, wind-whipped day in Cleveland, the Chargers overcame the weather and the Browns to clinch the AFC West, their first divisional title in a decade.

"It's an unbelievable feeling," said Tomlinson, who

had run for 111 yards and a pair of TDs on the snow-covered field. "I'm overjoyed. I've been waiting a long time to get to the playoffs, and now it's finally going to be happening."

A few days after that win, the NFL announced that Tomlinson, Brees, and Gates had been selected for the AFC's Pro Bowl roster. It was a big step up from last year when the Chargers didn't send a single player to Hawaii, where the NFL's all-star game is played.

"I was more excited for Drew," said LT. "He stuck in there through all the hard times he went through last year, and just kept believing in himself."

The Bolts, who had won eight straight games, were finally upended when the Indianapolis Colts beat them in an overtime thriller, 34-31. LT managed to put his name in the record book, again, by scoring a touchdown in his 12th straight game, which broke the single-season mark of 11 that had been set by Emmitt Smith in 1995 and tied by Kansas City's Priest Holmes in 2002.

But the day belonged to the Colts' Peyton Manning, whose 49th touchdown pass of 2004 helped send the game into OT, and broke the record of 48 that had been set in 1984 by Hall of Famer Dan Marino.

The Bolts closed out the season with a win against Kansas City, finishing the season with a 12-4 record, the exact mirror image of 2003, when they had finished 4-12. LT, meanwhile, was chafing at the bit for his first playoff action.

"It's an opportunity that I've been waiting for since I was drafted," said Tomlinson, who had finished the season with 1,335 rushing yards and 17 touchdowns, despite how his groin injury had slowed him down for a quarter of the season. "I'm really excited to see what the playoff atmosphere is all about."

The Bolts' opponent for their first playoff game in nine years was the Jets, the team that had outscored them in the second game of the season. The New Yorkers, however, had struggled down the stretch, while San Diego had soared, so the Chargers were confident of turning the tables on their East Coast visitors.

But it was the Jets who flew home with the win, a 20-17 overtime victory that burst the Bolt's playoff bubble.

Although Tomlinson was terribly disappointed by the unexpected loss and the Jets' ability to clamp down on the Chargers' high-scoring offense, he also had the maturity to put the season in a positive perspective.

"Nobody expected us to even make the playoffs, but we did," said LT. "And that's definitely something to build on."

11   OUTSIDE LOOKING IN

"Making the playoffs isn't a goal, it's an expectation," said LT, on the eve of the 2005 season. "I expect us to be in the playoffs and to be one of those teams that compete for a Super Bowl spot every year."

But the Bolts started the season by taking two steps backward, with losses to Dallas and Denver. Instead of building on what they had done in 2004, they played as if they could live off their prior accomplishments.

"It's still early," noted LT, who had set an NFL record by scoring a touchdown in his 14th consecutive game, breaking the mark that had been held by former stars John Riggins and George Rogers. "But 0-2 is pretty much the max. We have to do a better job than we have been doing."

Tomlinson then went out and set the example by rushing for 192 yards and three touchdowns, including a 65-yarder, in a 45-23 rout of the Giants. Tomlinson added to his picture perfect day by throwing a 26-yard touchdown strike to wide receiver Keenan McCardell, the second TD pass of his career.

"They worked me today," said LT, who toted the ball 21 times and also caught six passes. "Any time I'm sore, I'm happy."

The Bolts followed up the blowout of the Giants by pounding the Patriots 41-17, breaking New England's streak of 21 straight home wins. The 41 points were the most scored against the Pats in almost seven years, and the dominating effort against the defending Super Bowl champions had all the aspects of a coronation in the making.

"Beating the champs says a lot about this team," said Antonio Gates. "If we can beat the Pats, we can beat anyone."

But the Chargers stumbled in their very next game, a 24-22 loss to the Pittsburgh Steelers, before Tomlinson crafted another astonishing performance that led them to a 27-14 win over the Raiders. LT, who ran for 140 yards and had a hand in all three San Diego touchdowns, started the show by catching a 20-yard touchdown pass from Brees. It was the 18th straight game in which he had scored a touchdown, tying the record that had been set by Baltimore's Lenny Moore, who had had his streak from 1963-65.

"Lenny Moore is quite a guy and a Hall of Famer," said LT, who took the football back to the sideline for safekeeping. "That record had stood for 40 years, so I wanted a memento."

Later in the first half, LT scored on a 7-yard burst, which extended his own record of scoring a rushing TD to 18 straight games.

"He's the best in the league," said Raiders' linebacker Danny Clark. "Everyone knows that."

Then, shortly before halftime, Tomlinson took a handoff from Brees, ran to his right, and threw a 4-yard TD pass to Justin Peelle, becoming only the seventh player in NFL history to complete that scoring trifecta.

"I'm starting to worry about my job security," said Brees, with a smile. "He has the best quarterback rating in the history of the game."

But the Bolts had the smiles wiped off their faces the following week, when the Eagles beat them 20-17, held LT to a career-low seven rushing yards and stopped his scoring streak at 18.

"I'm disappointed at how we played, not about missing out on another record," said LT. "I've had a great run, and I don't mind at all being tied with Lenny. I'll take that any day."

Tomlinson had another relatively quiet day as the Bolts defeated Kansas City, which evened their record at 4-4 at the halfway mark of the season. But the following week, LT lit up the Jets at Giants Stadium for four touchdowns—one by air and three by ground—as the Bolts beat the Jets 31-26.

"It's difficult to put into words just what he means to this team," said Brees. "It's not only about what he does on the field, it's also about his leadership and the example that he sets with his work ethic. And when it comes to performance, there's not a more complete player in the league. Everyone knows about his running, catching and throwing the football, but he's also one of the best backs in the league—if not *the* best—at pass blocking."

The Bolts then blew out the Bills, 48-10, to run their modest winning streak to three games. And they won again the following week, 23-17, when LT ended the game in Washington with a 41-yard TD run in overtime. It was the third score of the game for Tomlinson, who had tied the game with a 32-yard jaunt with just 3:29 left in regulation time.

"I've said it before, but I don't mind saying it again; he's the finest running back I've ever seen," said Schottenheimer.

"I appreciate his support, but Coach may be a little biased," said Tomlinson, with a smile and a shrug, when told of Schottenheimer's assessment. "Hopefully, by the time I hang up my cleats, a lot of other people will feel that way. But I still have a long way to go, and a lot more to prove."

The Bolts ran their winning streak to five with a 34-10 rout of the Raiders, which upped their record to 8-4, and put them in prime position for a second straight playoff appearance. But LT suffered an injury during the game, a painful blow to the chest that would render him ineffective for the four games remaining on the Chargers' schedule. With their best player unable to operate at even close to full throttle, the Bolts sputtered to the finish line, losing three of those four games.

Ironically, their only victory in that stretch was a 26-17 win in Indianapolis, which spoiled the perfect season of the Colts, who had come into the game with a 13-0 record.

"We didn't come in with a mission to stop their streak," said Brees. "We were playing to make the playoffs and win a championship."

But the Bolts' 9-7 record left them on the outside looking in at the playoff picture, feeling as though they had let a golden opportunity slip through their fingers.

Despite the injury, Tomlinson posted another standout season, as he ran for 1,462 yards and 18 touchdowns, caught 51 passes for 370 yards and a pair of TDs, and also threw a trio of touchdown passes. The 20 touchdowns that he scored set a new Chargers' record, breaking the single-season mark of 19 that had been set by Chuck Muncie in 1981. LT had also upped his total of career yards from scrimmage to 9,755, eclipsing the team record that had been established by Lance Alworth.

But LT would have traded all of the 13 Charger records that he held, and his second straight selection to the Pro Bowl, for another shot at the playoffs.

12   A MOST ASTONISHING SEASON

In the wake of their late-season collapse, Chargers' general manager A.J. Smith decided to initiate a major shake-up. The changeover wasn't limited to players, but also involved assistant coaches, including the offensive line coach, who was blamed for his unit's inability to consistently open holes for LT and pass-block for Drew Brees.

The most significant changing of the guard occurred at the quarterback position, as Brees signed with the New Orleans Saints and was replaced by Philip Rivers, a 2004 first-round draft pick. The departure of Brees and his replacement by an untested quarterback created a sense of uncertainty among fans and even among some players. Sensing a potential problem, Tomlinson stood up and asked everyone to have patience and give Rivers and the team the opportunity to show what they could do in 2006.

"Drew is a great player and he was a great teammate and leader, and I know he'll transform the Saints," said Tomlinson. "But Philip's the quarterback now, and I know he's all about wanting to win and doing what's best for the team. I say if we don't win this season, then the fans will have a right to be upset. But give us a chance to prove that we are winners."

The team rewarded LT's show of faith by winning three of their first four games, despite unevenness by

Rivers, and even sub-par stats from Tomlinson. With a quarter of the season already gone, LT had scored only three times and amassed only 336 rushing yards, not many more than his backup, Michael Turner, who had run for 277 yards. But Tomlinson was about to begin a remarkable record-setting journey that would power the Chargers to the best record in the NFL.

LT took the first step of that trip by rushing for four touchdowns for the first time in his NFL career, as the Bolts blew out the San Francisco 49ers 48-19.

While the team stumbled to its second and last loss of the regular season the following week against Kansas City, 30-27, LT made it close by taking a Rivers pass into the end zone before adding another score on his fourth career TD toss. Although Tomlinson had been piling up points at a fairly rapid pace, he hadn't rushed for 100 yards since the first game of the season.

"It's tough to run now, with teams geared up to take away that aspect of our game," explained LT, who was about to start a streak of nine straight 100-yard games. "But as Philip starts to enjoy some more success passing, defenses will have to react and I'll start to have some big games on the ground."

LT began the roll by racking up 183 rushing yards against the Rams, which allowed him to tie Walter Payton as the seventh-fastest running back to reach 8,000 yards in a career.

"I've never been one to dwell too much on records and milestones, because I think that if you do that, you can start to get satisfied, and that's not what I'm about," said Tomlinson. "I'll pat myself on the back at the end of my career."

Tomlinson kept up the beat by busting through the Cleveland Browns defense for 172 yards and another three scores. At the halfway point of the season, the Bolts had a 6-2 record and LT, who was leading the league with 14 touchdowns, and second in rushing with 828 yards, began to hear the "MVP" chants echoing through Qualcomm Stadium.

"It's not something I even want to think about now, because it's just the middle of the season," said LT. "Let's see where things are at when it's all over."

The Bolts started the second half of the season with one of the most exciting comebacks in NFL history, as they rallied from a 28-7 halftime deficit to beat the Bengals in Cincinnati, 49-41.

"It happened so fast that it almost seemed like a video game," said Tomlinson, who rushed for 104 yards and four TDs. "But we believed that once we got it going, we could win the game, and you need to have belief in yourselves."

The Chargers dug themselves another deep hole the following week, when they trailed at Denver 24-7 early in the third quarter. But Tomlinson pulled them up and out by scoring four more touchdowns, as the Bolts rallied to beat the Broncos, 35-27, to take over the division lead.

Those four scores allowed Tomlinson to total 100 touchdowns in only his 89th game, four games faster than the previous record holders, Emmitt Smith and Hall of Famer Jim Brown, who many people consider to be the greatest running back of all time.

"Just to be mentioned in the same sentence with Jim Brown is a big deal to me," said LT. "It's one of the big things that later on in life I'll be able to brag to my kids about. But I can't take all the credit; it's an entire team effort. The offensive line has been great and Lorenzo Neal is the best blocking back in the league. I'm just going along for the ride."

In the following game, Tomlinson put the team on his back, as he sandwiched two scoring runs around a 19-yard TD pass to Gates, which lifted the Chargers over the Raiders, 21-14. The Bolts then went to Buffalo and beat the Bills 24-21, as LT rushed for two touchdowns and racked up 178 yards on the ground, to join Hall of Famer Eric Dickerson as only the second player in NFL history to rush for 1,200 yards or more in each of his first six seasons in the league.

Tomlinson crossed the 1,200-yard mark with style, ripping off a 51-yard TD run late in the first quarter behind a thunderous block by Lorenzo Neal, who created enough space for a mid-sized car to move through.

"Sometimes, LT just leaves you breathless," said Gates. "He makes so many extraordinary plays so consistently that you run out of words to describe him."

The Bolts returned to Qualcomm for their next game and battered the Broncos, 48-20, to clinch the AFC West for the second time in three years. And LT continued to leave teammates searching for words and tacklers grasping at air by rushing for a trio of scores. The three TDs gave him a record-setting 29 touchdowns for the year, eclipsing the 28 scores that Seattle running back Shaun Alexander had totaled in 2005.

As soon as LT scored the record-setting TD, his offensive linemen rushed over to him and two of them, Mike Goff and Kris Dielman, hoisted Tomlinson on to their shoulders.

"The thing I'll remember most is looking back and seeing those guys running toward me," said LT, who had, amazingly, scored 26 of the TDs in just a nine-game span. "That was phenomenal, because they had more to do with the record than I did. Obviously, people look at me scoring touchdowns but, man, the guys on the line make sure we get in the end zone.

"When we're old and can't play this game anymore, these are the moments we'll remember and be able to tell our kids and grandchildren about. We'll be able to talk about something special that we did. Today, we made history."

Tomlinson continued to make history in the Bolts' next game, when he scored two more touchdowns and upped his point total for the season to 186, breaking the record for points in a season that had been set in 1960 by Hall of Fame running back and place-kicker, Paul Hornung.

Although Tomlinson didn't score any more touchdowns in the team's final two regular-season games, he did go on to win his first rushing title, with 1,815 yards, and also captured the NFL MVP Award, completing one of the most astonishing seasons ever compiled by a football player.

"I would feel so much better about winning these individual honors if we would win the Super Bowl," said Tomlinson. "That would make it all feel perfect."

Unfortunately for LT, the Bolts didn't make it past their first playoff game, losing to the Patriots, 24-21. Although Tomlinson scored two of their three TDs and set up the third by catching a short screen pass and turning it into a 58-yard gain, it wasn't enough to overcome a

Tom Brady-led fourth-quarter comeback by New England.

"I don't know what to say," said LT, who had totaled 187 yards, 123 on the ground. "The disappointment is overwhelming, and I don't know if I can put it into words."

13   THE ROAD AHEAD

A month after the loss to the Patriots, Tomlinson suffered a much greater hurt when his father died in an automobile crash.

"It's a part of life, but you never expect it," said Tomlinson, who had reconnected with his father in the past few years. "You think your parents will live forever, but that's not realistic. All I have now are the memories of the things he taught me and the good times we had."

During his first six seasons in the NFL, Tomlinson has created a different set of memories for people who watch and play the game. He's already established himself as one of the greatest running backs in the history of the game, and as a definite candidate for the Hall of Fame. At his current pace, he would break both Emmitt Smith's career rushing record and Jerry Rice's career touchdown mark of 208 in his twelfth season.

"LaDainian Tomlinson is a remarkable, remarkable player," said Hall of Fame running back Marcus Allen. "He has a chance to rewrite all the records."

But LT doesn't gaze that far down the road, any more than he looks back at what he's already accomplished.

"I'm focused on the present right now," said LT. "I just want to build something special and, when it's all done I'll look back and see what I did. But it's way too early to think about my place in history or the Hall of Fame."

But what Tomlinson brings to the game can't be measured solely in terms of records or achievements, past or future.

"Someday, when I'm an old man, I'll tell my kids that I played with the Great One," said Lorenzo Neal. "And he's a better man and teammate than he is a player. I think that should be considered greatness, too."

One measure of Tomlinson the man was reflected in his being named the co-winner, along with Drew Brees, of the 2006 Walter Payton Man of the Year Award. The award, which honors the late running back, is based on a player's charity work in the community, as well as his performance on the field.

Tomlinson's efforts in the community include sponsoring an annual celebrity golf tournament, which raises scholarships for the LT School is Cool program. He has also set up the Tomlinson Touching Lives Foundation, which, among other things, delivers food to needy people at Thanksgiving and administers a college scholarship fund. Tomlinson also runs two football camps for children, one in San Diego and the other in Waco. Delivering on a promise that he had made to himself when he attended Emmitt Smith's camp more than fifteen years ago, LT doesn't charge a fee to the children who attend his camps.

"I'm not going to say that I'm going to change the world, but I do want to make a difference," said Tomlinson, who lives in the San Diego area with his wife, LaTorsha. "Playing football has put me in a position to influence people in a positive way, and I want to take advantage of that opportunity. But football isn't who I am. Football is what I do to earn a living."

ORDER FORM

If you enjoyed this book, you might want to order some of the other exciting titles written by Richard J. Brenner, the best-selling sportswriter in America.

QTY

BASEBALL SUPERSTARS ALBUM 2007: Includes 16 full-sized, full-color photos of 16 of the game's top players—including Derek Jeter, Albert Pujols, Ryan Howard, and Justin Morneau—plus biographical sketches and career stats. 48 pages, 8-1/2 x 11. $6.99 US.   _____

SUPERSTAR QUARTERBACKS: Includes biographical sketches and 18 full-color photos of six top quarterbacks: Peyton Manning, Eli Manning, Vince Young, Philip Rivers, Tony Romo and Drew Brees. 32 pages, 6 x 9. $3.99 US.   _____

TOM BRADY * LADAINIAN TOMLINSON: A dual-biography of two of the NFL's top players. The book includes 16 action-packed color photos. 144 pages, 5 x 8. $5.99 US.   _____

EXTREME ACTION STARS: Includes 15 action-packed photos and biographical sketches of Shaun White, Danny Way, Travis Pastrana, Bucky Lasek, and Blair Morgan. 32 pages, 8-1/2 x 11. $4.99 US.   _____

BRETT FAVRE: An easy-to-read photo-filled biography of one of football's all-time greats. Written especially for younger children. 32 pages, 8 x 8. $4.50 US.   _____

SPECIAL OFFER: The books listed below are being offered for $1.00 each, plus normal shipping charges.

MARK McGWIRE: An easy-to-read photo-filled biography of one of baseball's all-time greats. Written especially for younger children. 32 pages, 8 x 8. Originally published at $4.50 US.   _____

FOOTBALL'S SUPERSTAR ALBUM 2000: Includes 16 full-sized, full-color photos of 16 of the game's top players, plus biographical sketches and career stats. 48 pages, 8-1/2 x 11. Originally published at $4.99 US.   _____

Total Number of Book(s) Ordered   _____

Add $1.50 per book if you want book(s) autographed by author.   _____

Total Cost of Books   _____

TAX (NY State residents must add appropriate sales tax)   _____

Shipping Charges (in the US) $2.25 per book, up to a maximum of $11.25 on orders of 10 or fewer books.

TOTAL PAYMENT ENCLOSED: (All payments must be in US currency; checks and money orders only; credit cards not accepted).   _____

(Please print clearly.)

NAME _____

ADDRESS _____

CITY _____ STATE _____ ZIP CODE _____

SEND PAYMENTS TO: **EAST END PUBLISHING, LTD.**
112 Abbott Drive, Huntington, NY 11743.

Discounts are available on orders of 25 or more books.
For details write or email: rjbrenner1@gmail.com
Terms are subject to change without notice.